Geometric Pop-ups

Instructions, Techniques & Designs, Volume 1

by Guy Petzall

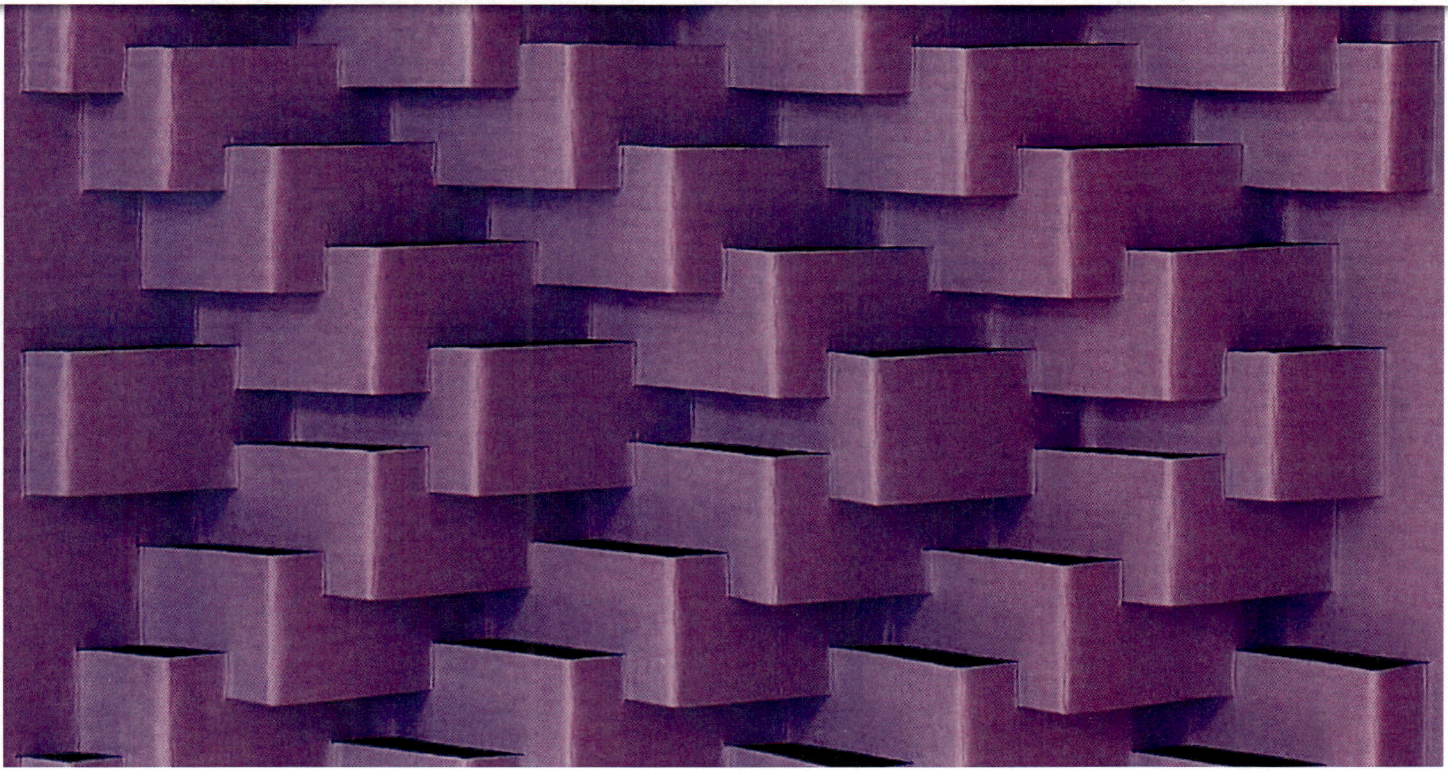

Copyright © 2020 by Guy Petzall, Ullagami and 1iTurtle, LLC

All rights reserved.

The templates in this book may be reproduced for personal use only, but may not be transmitted or distributed. The textual and photographic portions of this book or any portion thereof may not be reproduced or used in any manner whatsoever without the express written permission of the author.

Sixth Edition, 2020

ISBN 979-8-61846-762-9

- ullagami.com
- etsy.com/shop/Ullagami
- facebook.com/Ullagami
- @ullagami

Contents

What is Ullagami? 4
Tools 5
Papers and Cards 6
Construction 7
Framing and Presentation 14
The Templates 17

TEMPLATE GUIDE

3x3 Building Blocks 16	5x5 Building Blocks 16	5x5 Spiral 18
9x5 Hourglass 18	Eck Scross 20	Mandala 1 20
3x3 Obloid 22	5x5 Obloid 22	9x9 Diamond 24
9x9 ZigZag 26	9x9 Spiral 28	9x9 Meander 30
9x9 Meander2 32	Split Quarters 34	9x9 Obloid 36
9x9 Obloid ZigZag 38	9x9 Obloid Spiral 40	9x9 Obloid Whorl 42
Linked Meanders 44	Knights' Moves 46	Wavey 48
Meandered Spiral 50	Spiralink 52	Big Spiralink 54
Eddies' Droop 56		

What is Ullagami?

Ullapool, cut using survey map contour lines.

A few years ago my family and I moved to northern Scotland, where the winters are long and the nights seemingly without end. And so, in order to beguile the many hours of darkness, I began working with paper. I have been doing origami for over a decade, but here I quickly moved on to kirigami, fascinated by the possibilities I found available by interrupting the folded surfaces that origami generally likes to keep intact.

The parameters I set for myself were simple: each model should collapse folded flat when completed; and each model should be created from a single sheet of paper — nothing should be added or removed, but rather the surface of the paper should be rearranged without losing a shred of its area.

Beginning with simple building-block designs, the pieces evolved further and further within the limits of my basic parameters, and my manual and mathematical abilities.

The name Ullagami is a portmanteau; it is a mixture of origami and kirigami, and because the village I live in is called Ullapool. It wasn't until I decided to create a Japanese "chop" to stamp the backs of the pieces I was constructing that I learned, quite by surprise, that the transliteration of "ullagami" into Japanese is ウラガミ, which literally means "the back of the paper" — exactly where I wanted to put the stamp! Perfect! A very happy accident indeed.

(You can imagine how hard my palm hit my forehead when I proudly showed a Japanese friend my new stamp, and she said, "That's cute and very American. But we normally write it top-down and right-to-left."

D'oh! So I remade the stamp. Like everything else I design: you have to cut it, evaluate it, and then cut it again right.)

Of course I soon learned that these models fall loosely into the more general category of Origamic Architecture, but since OA includes a huge variety of crafts which, though often amazing, do not match specifically with my own purely geometric approach, I prefer to use the term Ullagami instead. And besides: it's a lot easier to say!

Basic Tools

At its simplest, you need only 5 tools to construct the models in this book: a cutting mat, a metal ruler, a scoring tool, a scalpel, and some adhesive. For each tool, the choice is subjective, but for the purpose of constructing the models in this book, here's a brief discussion of what seems to work best.

Glue stick ~ For attaching your template to the card below.

Cutting mat ~ These come in a range of sizes and materials, from spongy rubber to hard glass. If the mat is too supple, your score lines will sink quite deeply into the card, and your cuts can become less accurate as the mat grips the blade and provides too much resistance. Conversely, a really hard mat can make it difficult to make meaningful score lines at all, while the blade can slide almost too fast to control. Look instead for something in the middle, which suits your natural working pressure and works with the type of card or paper you most like to use. Whatever mat you choose, always be sure to store it flat, and keep it clean.

Ruler ~ A metal ruler is essential for guiding your other tools along neat, straight lines. For our purposes you'll need one at least a page tall, i.e. 30cm, although additional smaller rulers can come in handy for finer work.

Ballpoint Pen ~ For scoring future fold lines. The traditional tool for this job is the embossing point, but a ballpoint pen is arguably a better scoring tool; it rolls, rather than drags, across your template, with the added benefit that it's easy to see which lines you've already scored. Get the finest point you can find, and look for one with dry ink that won't soak through your template and mark the card below.

Scalpel ~ There is a surprising array of scalpel handles available, so it really comes down to what you find most comfortable. Regarding the blades themselves, the key for Ullagami is a good sharp point; the majority of the sharpened edge never gets used. So avoid blades that are rounded or flat. Standard #11 blades, which are cheap and easily available, always work well.

Papers and Cards

There is such a dazzling variety of papers and cards out there that it's really quite a thrill to experiment and play with different types. But there are some general pointers which can be useful when deciding which paper to use.

The basic parameters guiding your choice of card are weight, texture and color.

Since papers have different densities, the weight of a paper (usually labeled in grams or pounds) doesn't always tell you how thick it is. There is quite a range of thicknesses for 150gsm paper, for example. For sharp tidy folds, thinner paper is better within the same weight range.

Put most simply, heavier papers offer more structure but can be bulky and clumsy; while lighter papers allow for greater accuracy, elegance, and workability, but at the expense of strength. It's always a balance: since the models in this book need to hold themselves up, you want a paper that's rigid enough to support its own weight, while at the same time remaining sharp and fine, with crisp, neat folds. Experiment to find what works best for you, but as a general pointer, all the images in this book use paper stocks between 150 and 200 gsm (which stands for "grams per square meter" – a very useful measure!).

Also consider the humidity of the environment in which you live. Humidity makes all papers wilt... if you live in a very humid place, stiffer paper will fare better.

Texture can also make a big difference in your final pieces. Depending upon the scale and color of the models you cut, gently textured papers can flatten glare and deepen shadows, contributing to an overall richness in appearance. However, textured paper has drawbacks as well, primarily a sacrifice in the sharpness of the folds you can make. Bumpier paper = messier folds. Many of the photographed models in this book were made using very slightly textured stocks, so again, look for a balance that suits the final look you're going for, and most importantly that feels good to work with.

The color you choose for your models also has a huge impact on the final result. The same model sometimes looks quite different when cut in different colors. For the most drama, brighter colors do a good job of maximizing the play between shadow and light. In other cases, darker paper choices result in a mellower, less confrontational appearance.

But while careful color selection can really affect the "mood" of a model, never underestimate the enduring beauty and simplicity of plain white card.

Regardless of all the many papers you may find to experiment with, you will also likely need a stack of normal vanilla white card to play with. For drafts, experiments, trial runs, and explorations, you can find cheap white card at any stationers' store.

So now we've discussed the materials and the tools, it's time to start making something with them...

Construction

If you've already had some experience with kirigami and origamic architecture, then the basic instructions I typically supply to people who want to try my designs read as follows:

> 1. Print the template onto regular paper. 2. Tape or very lightly glue-stick one edge of the template to the card. 3. Through the paper into the card, score all the fold lines with an embossing point or a ball-point pen. 4. Cut all the cut lines with a scalpel. 5. Inspect the back to make sure it all looks right. 6. Remove the template from the card. 7. Using your fingers, reinforce all the scored creases in their proper directions. 8. Gently massage the piece into its final form. The whole thing collapses flat when it's finished. Good luck!

That's really all there is to it. Sounds simple, right? And if you're comfortable with that, feel free skip the rest of this text and jump right to the templates later on in this book. However, having watched many people learn to cut my designs, with all different levels of experience and skill, I have seen many of the mistakes, pitfalls and missed intuitions that can naturally occur. So a more detailed description of (what I consider to be) the best methods and practices for constructing these designs, please read on.

For teaching and diagrammatic purposes, We will use the "5x5 building blocks" model which is available on page 16, and also at ullagami.com, along with a short video demonstrating how to make it. It's a simple enough model to learn on, while just complex enough to reveal the techniques required by some of the more advanced designs. Once you get the hang of it, the basic method for all the Ullagami models, regardless of difficulty level, is more or less the same.

Also it's worth noting that the instructions that follow are not set in stone. Everyone has their own intuitions and preferences; here we'll merely discuss certain tried-and-true methods that work reliably.

Step 1: Preparation

Before you do anything else, make sure you have everything you need. These constructions require a little bit of focus and concentration, and having all your tools and materials assembled from the start is a good idea. Put a fresh blade in your scalpel. Wipe down your cutting mat. In fact (and here's a really good trick), close your eyes and lightly feel the entire surface of your cutting mat with your fingertips. This is more important than it sounds: when tips break off of scalpel blades, they often lie in ambush, embedded in the surface of the mat, waiting for another scalpel blade to come along and break too. Feeling the mat with eyes closed helps you find any of these little land mines before they can get in the way of your construction.

With all the matériel ready to go, the next step is to photocopy the template onto a sheet of normal white copy paper the same size as the card you want to use for your model. Make sure you mash the book as flat as possible onto the copier glass, to avoid distortion. All the models in this book are formatted to work on either A4- or Letter-sized paper, and all are completely scalable, either vertically, horizontally, or entirely. The templates are in color, but photocopying is fine: they work equally well in black and white.

Then attach the template to the card, using your glue stick. It's surprising how little glue you need: just the barest edge, a millimeter or two at most, across the top of the card will hold the template in place quite nicely. Some glue sticks even come in colors which dry clear, so you can see exactly how much you apply. You want to use enough glue to ensure that the template doesn't slip, but minimal enough to allow the two sheets to easily separate later on. A single glue stick can last more than a year, even if you do this *a lot*.

Once the template is attached to the card, place it on your mat, and you're ready to start.

> *Quick tip:* never use your cutting mat as a gluing surface. A piece of scrap paper (or your most recently cut template) will protect your cutting mat from getting sticky.

Step 2: Scoring.

It's worth mentioning at the start that the term "score" can actually have two meanings in this context. Scoring can mean "cutting lightly through the topmost layer of the paper's surface" (some people even use the back of a scalpel blade for this purpose); or it can alternatively mean "compressing the paper in a sharp line without breaking the surface of the paper at all." This book uses the term in that second sense: it's better to compress the paper than to lightly cut it, so it doesn't split along the folds. And now we return to or originally scheduled program:

When you bend or stress a piece of card enough to fold it, it looks for a natural place to "break." Depending upon the thickness and fiber of the card, these natural break-points can be unpredictable and untidy, as the card seeks to crease along the path of least resistance. It is therefore necessary to pre-score the card using a pointed tool, such as an embossing point or a ball-point pen, laying out the fault-lines, so that later when it's time to fold the model into its final shape, all the folds break precisely and neatly where you need them to be. This process of pre-scoring a card gives it a map of lines along which to naturally fold by itself, a path of least resistance which you control and provide, making the folding process much easier.

Every score in this book is a straight line, which makes this part of the construction relatively simple. Using your ruler, line up the template lines (which are always dotted lines) you want to score and, one at a time, drag your scoring tool precisely along each, pushing hard enough to make a clear and sharp indentation in the card, but not so hard that you cut through the template with your point. Then reposition your ruler on the next line to score and do it again, until all the dotted lines have been scored.

After all the dotted- and dashed lines have been scored, you can see from the underside of the card a neat pattern of ridges where the scoring tool has passed. All the fold lines are ready for the folding stage later on. But first we have some cutting to do...

A few tips on scoring:

- **If it's any kind of dotted line on the template, score it.** At this stage, mountain- and valley-folds are treated identically. They all score exactly the same.

- **Rely on your ruler.** Pressed firmly down onto the template, let the ruler guide your scoring tool along the page. It's the surest way to make the straightest, cleanest lines.

- **Work in the right direction, and only in one direction.** On models where the score lines lie parallel to the glued edge, always start at the glued side of the template and move *away* from the attached edge. If you begin at a free (unattached) edge and work toward the attachment, the template can tend to ripple and bunch up atop the card, which doesn't help the accuracy of your work. By progressing always away from the glued edge, the ruler will smooth out the template as you go.

- **Work systematically.** You don't want to miss out any of the score lines, only to discover too late that there are missing scores. The best way to avoid this is to move the ruler from one side of the page to the other, catching every score line it passes.

- **When possible, line up the score lines together.** In many of the models in this book, the score lines fall in collinear groups. You can line up your ruler across several at a time, which also helps ensure that it is at precisely the right angle when scoring.

- **Use constant speed and pressure.** The smoother and less "lumpy" your score lines are, the neater the folds they create will ultimately be.

- **Don't move the card on the mat, just move the whole mat.** The more you shift the template and card around relative to the mat, the more chance there is that they might wrinkle or buckle, or god forbid detach. If you need to adjust the positioning of the template relative to your hands or tools, it's better to move the whole cutting mat, keeping the card in its fixed position on top.

Step 3: Cutting

In a funny way, this step is both parallel and perpendicular to the scoring process. Again using your ruler, progress systematically across the page from one edge to the other, cutting through all the solid lines with the point of your scalpel. The general method for this is *point, sink, drag, lift*. Position the point of the blade on the starting end of the cut you want to make, and plunge it gently but firmly downward, through the template and card, and into the mat. You can feel a small tactile thud as it pierces through. Then smoothly drag the blade along the cut-line, to the end, and finally lift the scalpel out, straight up. Many of the techniques from the scoring stage also apply here: work away from the attached edge, work systematically from one side to the other, line up collinear cuts with your ruler, and use steady speed and pressure when moving the blade through the card.

> **More tips for cutting:**
>
> - **Use enough pressure, but not too much.** Firm hand, light touch. The pressure should be enough to cut cleanly through the template and the card, without going overboard: the deeper the blade sinks into the mat, the less accurate your cuts will be, as the width of the scalpel increases away from its tip. Cut through the template and the card, but try not to scar the mat. If you find you have a habit of pressing too hard, it might help to print your templates on slightly thicker paper.
>
> - **Keep the blade as vertical as possible.** In the interest of precision and control, the more upright you keep the blade when it enters the paper, the less metal will actually enter the surface of the paper and card, resulting in sharper, more accurate cuts. It's also easier to see what you're doing when the blade is out of your way. Only the tip, and never the long edge, of the scalpel, should ever come into contact with the paper.
>
> - **Always recap the blade when it's not in your hand.** Simple, stupid advice, but sometimes it's quite convenient to just set the blade down without re-capping it. Those things are sharp, you know. Make capping the blade second nature when you put it down, it's a safe habit to have. And these models look better without blood on them.

Step 4: Inspect, Disconnect, Inspect Again

After you have finished scoring and cutting all the lines in the pattern, turn the template and card over, and lay them, still connected, on the cutting mat. This is your chance to inspect your work before detaching the template from the card. Once the template is detached, it's nigh impossible to get it realigned properly with the card. Have a close look at the template in good light. Make sure all the cuts went through properly, nd that they fully connect where they intersect. Make sure that there are no scores or cuts which are missing from the pattern. After you've had a little experience and practice, you should be able to spot missing elements quite easily, but as a general rule, no cut or score should ever end without another cut or score connecting to and continuing it. If you see a cut or score line that just ends by itself, it's a good indicator that there's something missing.

Once you're sure that all the scores and cuts are in place, you can disconnect the template from the card. There are two ways to do this. Most directly, you can simply peel the template away from the card, carefully so that there's no ripping or rippling (this is why you should use as little glue as possible). Alternatively, you can cut out along the frame lines which border the page. Every template in this book has frame lines set a centimeter in from the edges of the page, and by cutting these lines, you also cut away the glued edge, freeing the card underneath. Make sure that you *cut the frame line closest to the glued edge last*, as it's holding the template in place for the other three cuts. Keep the template on hand for the next step, and throw away the rectangular frame of paper.

Now you have a pristine card, with the template etched into it. It's time to start the most satisfying part: folding your model.

Step 5: Folding

Here's where we turn a flat sheet of card into a 3D model. The first thing to know about this phase is that it's a gradual process. Since all the folds are interdependent, it's not possible to make them 90° one at a time, without stressing the paper. If we could fold them all simultaneously, then we could just collapse the whole thing at once, but in the real word the trick is to systematically and repeatedly increase all their angles, bit by bit, until the each of the folds reaches its final position.

> A quick note about the different types of fold-lines in these templates: There are three kids of fold-lines marked. A "mountain" fold (dashed lines, in blue) angles away from the paper and toward you, like a mountain. A "valley" fold (dotted lines, in red) points the opposite way, away from the viewer and toward the background page. The "spine" folds (small dotted lines, green)are really just valley folds, but the spine is the central fold of the whole model, separating the wall from the floor, so it is marked slightly differently.

To start, begin by "puffing out" the central design from the surrounding paper, lifting the model away from its background, as follows: first, fold the spine lines. There are usually only ever two of these lines, which extend from the edges of the central design to the edges of the card. This spine is actually the primary fold for the whole model: it is what separates the floor from the wall, so to speak. Using your fingers, pinch-crease these two lines so that they fold to a 90° angle.

Next, work your way around the borders of the design with your fingers, gently popping the whole central section away from the surrounding card. The cuts should lift away cleanly, and where there are scores around the edges of the model, delicately start to fold them. Don't worry about making them sharp 90° angles yet — they won't hold that angle until the other folds are done too — but by gently guiding the card to fold along these score lines, you begin the process, and you can see the model start to lift away from its background. Go all the way around, until you have a sort of "pillow" of card raised away from the surrounding surface.

Now comes the tricky part: working systematically through the model, nudge each score line into a fold in its appropriate direction, either mountain or valley. After a bit of experience it will become clear which lines will ultimately become mountain folds and which valleys, but you can always use the template you started with as a guide. It's generally easiest to begin with the biggest folds on the page, which are usually mountain folds.

Working from both the front and back of the card, push out from behind these mountain folds with a fingertip, while gingerly pinching the line into a crease on the front side of the card with your other hand. Remember, the reason we scored the fold lines in the first place was to give the card a natural place to crease when flexed; this is where we do that flexing and creasing. They don't have to be 90° angles yet, we just need to show the card, one score line at a time, which way it should fold when the real crunch comes later on. One at a time, reinforce every crease on the page. As you go, the general form of the final model should start to emerge. It's tricky and time-consuming, but this step is important: if all the folds are given a proper start, there will be no ambiguity when the final folding happens, and as a result, there will be no warping or ripples in the final model.

Be methodical and consistent. For most models, it's best to work from the edges in toward the center, but ultimately the order in which you approach the folds is less important than making sure you get them all. For creases that are too small for your fingertips, you can always use a tool to help you, and also remember you can work on both sides of the card, pinching the mountains from the front, and the valleys from behind.

After all the folds have been initially guided, each in its proper direction, go back and work through them all again, increasing their sharpness. Depending upon the model, this might take a few passes, incrementally nudging all the folds toward their proper conclusions. But once you're satisfied that they all know where to go, then it's time for the final crunch.

The goal now is to get the entire model to fold along the spine, and collapse flat upon itself. Place the card's bottom edge flat upon the table and gently angle the spine toward 90°. This will put some pressure on all the lines we scored and folded. Keeping that pressure steady, start with the bottom-most block, and collapse it forward until its top lies flat upon its face. Then do the same with the next row of blocks. And again. As you progress farther away from the bottom row this will become more difficult; sometimes it's tricky to get a physical grip upon the surfaces you want to work on, but be patient and, row by row, they should fold flat.

If you notice any of the scored folds resisting collapse, you might need to occasionally pause and revisit some of the individual folds and once again nudge them in their proper directions as you go. When it gets frustrating, or when you get near the center of the model, turn the whole thing around, and start from the top down using the same techniques.

Eventually, the centermost rows of the model will be the only ones left un-collapsed. At this final stage, if they don't seem like they'll easily fall into place by themselves (which does happen occasionally), it can sometimes be effective to grip the whole card almost like a sandwich, applying pressure from both the top and bottom, and gently squeeze until the whole card folds flat.

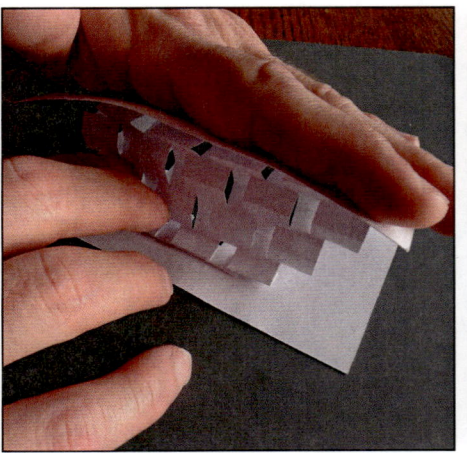
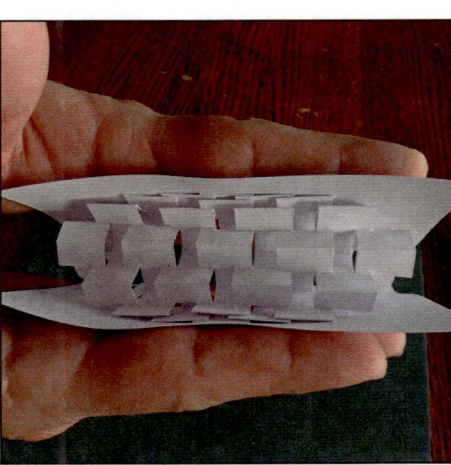
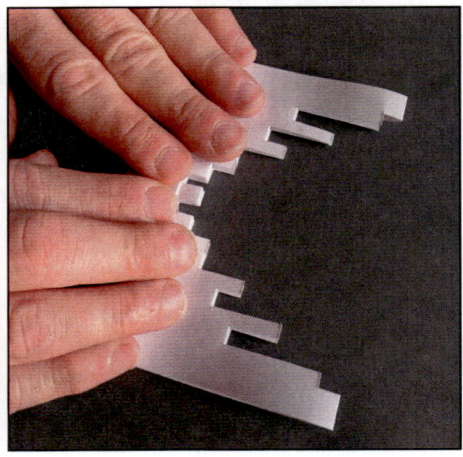

And finally, the best part: from its completely collapsed state, peel the card open like a book, until the spine is once more at a 90° angle. And there's your model! The only thing left now is to look it over and re-crease any folds that don't seem sharp enough, making sure that every fold is at last a right angle. Then turn it over, and do the same with the valley folds from the back. And voila! Your model is complete!

(Step 6: Do it again)

If your final model has extra creases and wrinkles, ripples or small tears, don't be discouraged. Even with loads of practice, it's rare to make a model perfectly the first time. So think of the first try as a familiarization process, learning which bits are trickiest and where you could be more careful. Certainly with some of the more complex designs in this book, it has taken several attempts before achieving a perfect result. But perfection is possible, with just a little more practice.

A few more leftover (yet important) general tips:

- **You watch a complete demonstration for constructing this model on YouTube.** It takes about 15 minutes, and includes thorough descriptions of technique all the way through. Look for it using the search term "Ullagami."

- **Surrender yourself to a certain amount of imperfection.** This is supposed to be relaxing, not stressful. Keep the inaccuracies and imperfections to a minimum, of course, but don't get flustered if something goes wrong. It's only paper.

- **Feel the paper as you go.** Not to get all Obi-Wan on you, but feeeeeeel. With enough experience you should be able to feel the texture and the fiber of both the template and the card beneath, through the point, as it drags along the template. With this sensitivity, you will learn to score and cut neat, even lines that start and end precisely. And not to get all Yoda on you, but eventually you will be able to feel the differences between different cards, different types of cutting mats, and even different table surfaces, all through the scoring tool and the scalpel. Even the sounds different papers make when you work with them will help you understand the textures and fibres you're working with.

- **Use the right size ruler for the job.** Cutting and scoring across the width of an A4- or letter-sized card, use a 20cm ruler, and then switch to the 30cm to work vertically on the same sheet. The reason for this is two-fold: you want a tool that is long enough for the purpose without being so long that it gets in your way; and also if the ruler more or less fits the whole length or width of the page, it does a better job of gripping without warping the surface, which in turn helps to keep the template and the card together and where you want them to be.

- **Don't work at the big shared table at the coffeehouse.** It shakes when people use it.

- **Have a safe system for your discarded blades.** The old blades can pile up quickly, and they're still razor sharp. This makes them difficult to just throw into the bin, as they easily slice through any trash bag. By keeping a small, solid container on hand, like an old Tic-Tac box, for example, you can safely collect them for later disposal when the box gets full. Or, alternatively, consider using a wine cork: with enough blades, you can make a very handsome hedgehog!

Framing and Presentation

There are as many ways of framing Ullagami models as stars in the sky. But for the purposes of this discussion, let's stick with simple paper frames, since ultimately it's all about the simplicity of paper.

Every template in this book is set within a cutaway border 1cm from the edge of the page. By removing that border from your finished piece, it is easy to frame your model against another piece of card the same size as your original sheet. Not only does this make your finished piece look nicer by providing color contrast and perhaps a sense of "framedness," but it can structurally help the model maintain its shape by providing a back-board, fortifying the model against any sagging that gravity can sometimes naturally cause. Of course a frame is not strictly necessary, and if the card you use to cut your models is rigid enough to stand on its own, you can freely skip this step. But sometimes it's nice to cut these models on lighter, more flexible paper; and having a colored model against a differently colored card can really make an impression.

To make the framing card, you can use the same template as the piece you're framing. Most importantly, *the frame and the model it contains must share a spine*, which is the primary fold upon which all these pieces are based. Many of the designs simply fold in half, but some of them have off-center or diagonal spines. Using the same template you used for the original model insures that the spines of your model and your frame line up correctly. Remember not to use any glue on your frame — just place the template on the card and score only the spine line as marked on the frame template.

Next, making certain that the template and your framing card are still perfectly aligned (remember, there's no glue to hold them together), carefully cut four corner slits through both the template and the card.

And finally, discard the template, and simply thread the four corners of your model into the slits in the frame.

Ta-Da!

Of course that there are lots of ways to customize and beautify your frame. You can double up the corner slits, making straps, so that the corners of your model remain visible on the front of the frame. You can cut those straps into curves, or whatever shape you like, to best frame your model. If your models have a tendency to sag due to overly thin paper or ambient humidity, you can cut darts of any shape and size to grip the model's edge in strategic positions. A dart cut into the frame at the spine will hold the model tightly to the framing card, and depending upon the piece you're making, adding darts can even enhance the final look of the piece.

And that's it! It's time to start cutting! The templates which follow start quite simple, and progress in complexity. With a little practice the most basic can be made, start to finish, in half an hour; the more complex models can take up to two hours to complete. Each is accompanied by a brief description of the concept behind its design, how it has evolved from the previous models, and any model-specific pointers and tips to help you cut.

Have fun, and as always: be careful with those blades!

 Templates

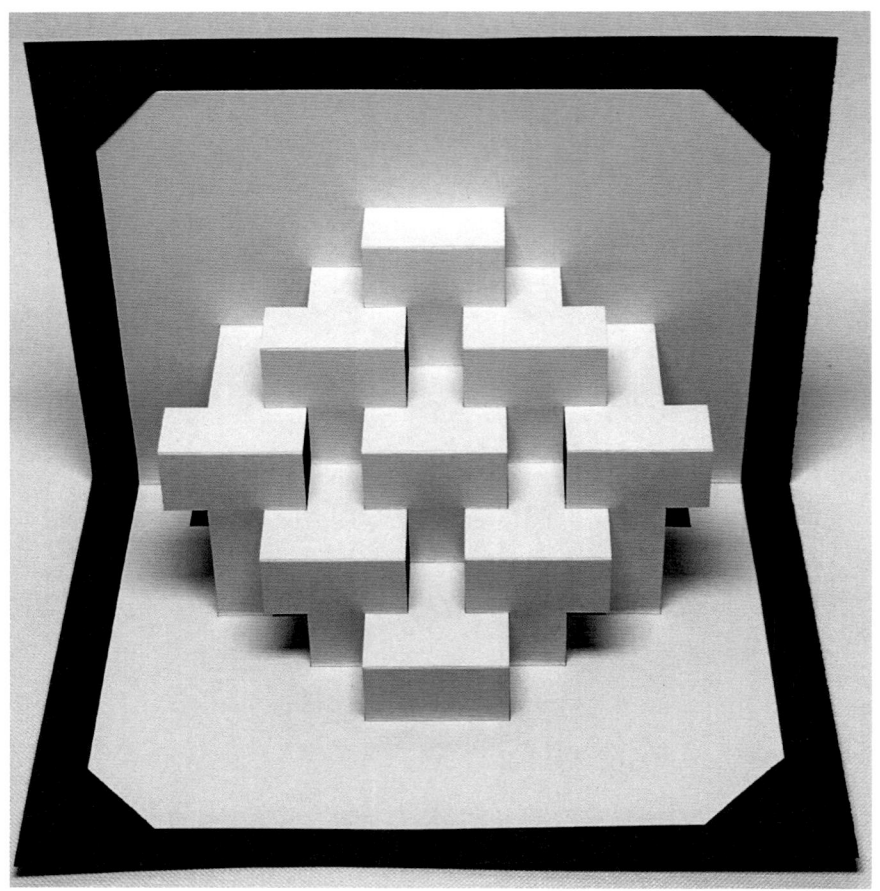

3x3 Building Blocks

Since all of the models in this book make use of the same basic principal of interlocking blocks, this simple 3x3 example is the best place to start.

5x5 Building Blocks

From 3x3 to 5x5, the complexity increases slightly, especially in the folding stage. But the ideas and techniques remain the same.

This is the model depicted in the how-to section.

3x3 Building Blocks

- cut
- mountain
- valley
- spine

5x5 Building Blocks

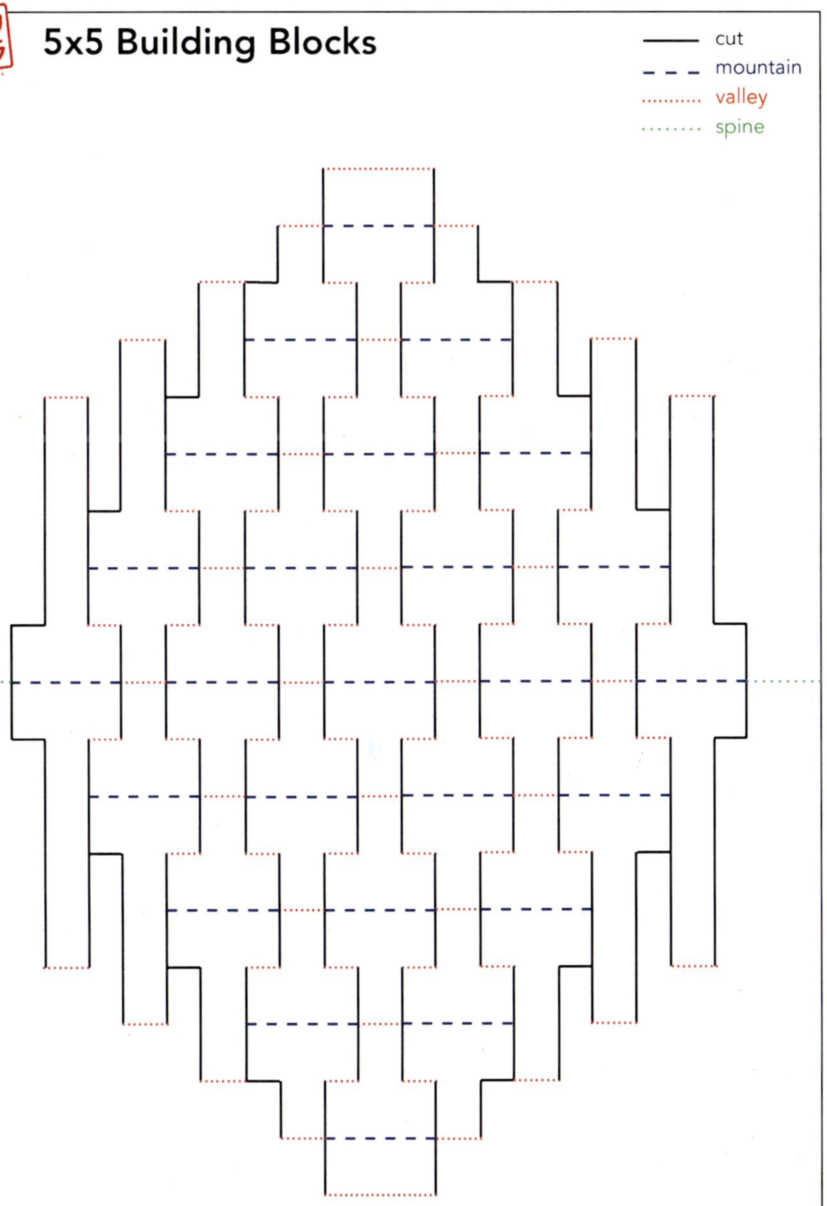

- cut
- mountain
- valley
- spine

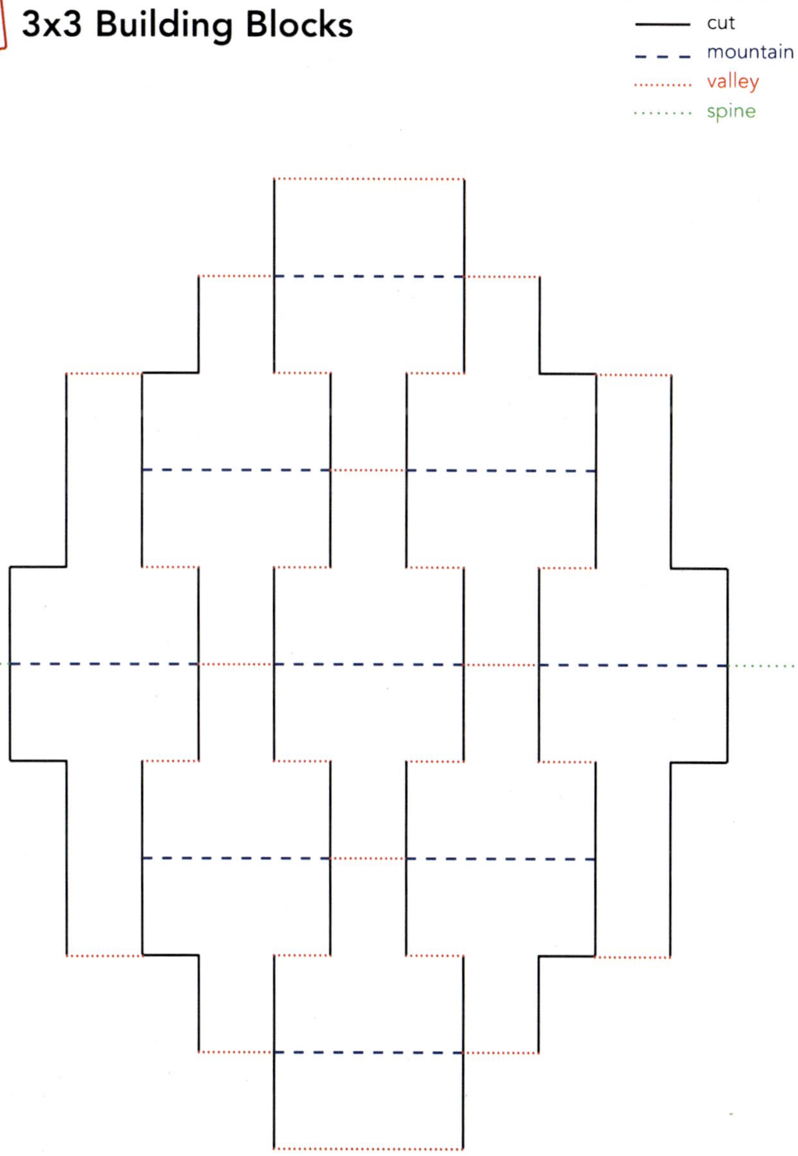

Conceived and designed by Guy Petzall ©2015. For more information, visit ullagami.com.

7x7 Spiral

Two slight steps up in complexity. A bigger grid, and with some steps removed to create a spiral pattern. Notice that there is a gentle variation in this model: the "arms" and "legs" which project from the model to the wall and floor are not notched in the same way as the previous designs. This slightly reduces the work of cutting, and gives the model a greater sense of solidity as though it has grown from, rather than merely being connected to, the page. Of course this sense of sturdiness sacrifices some elegance and lightness.

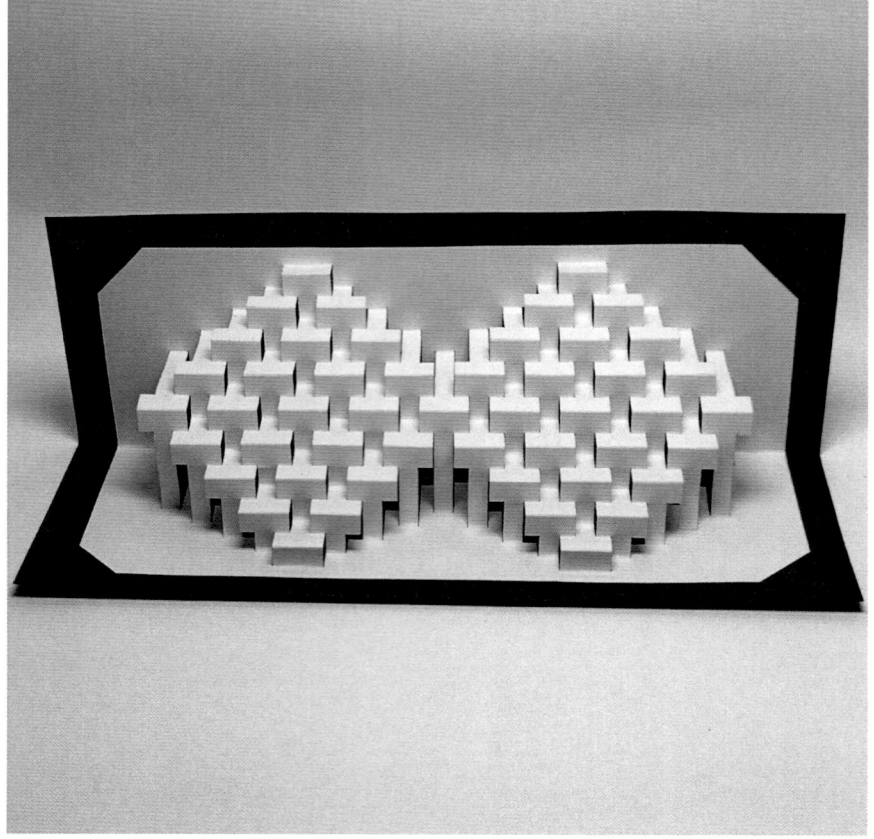

9x5 Hourglass

Given a field of blocks, any number of different shapes can be carved out. Here two 5x5 diamonds have been joined together.

7x7 Spiral

- cut
- mountain
- valley
- spine

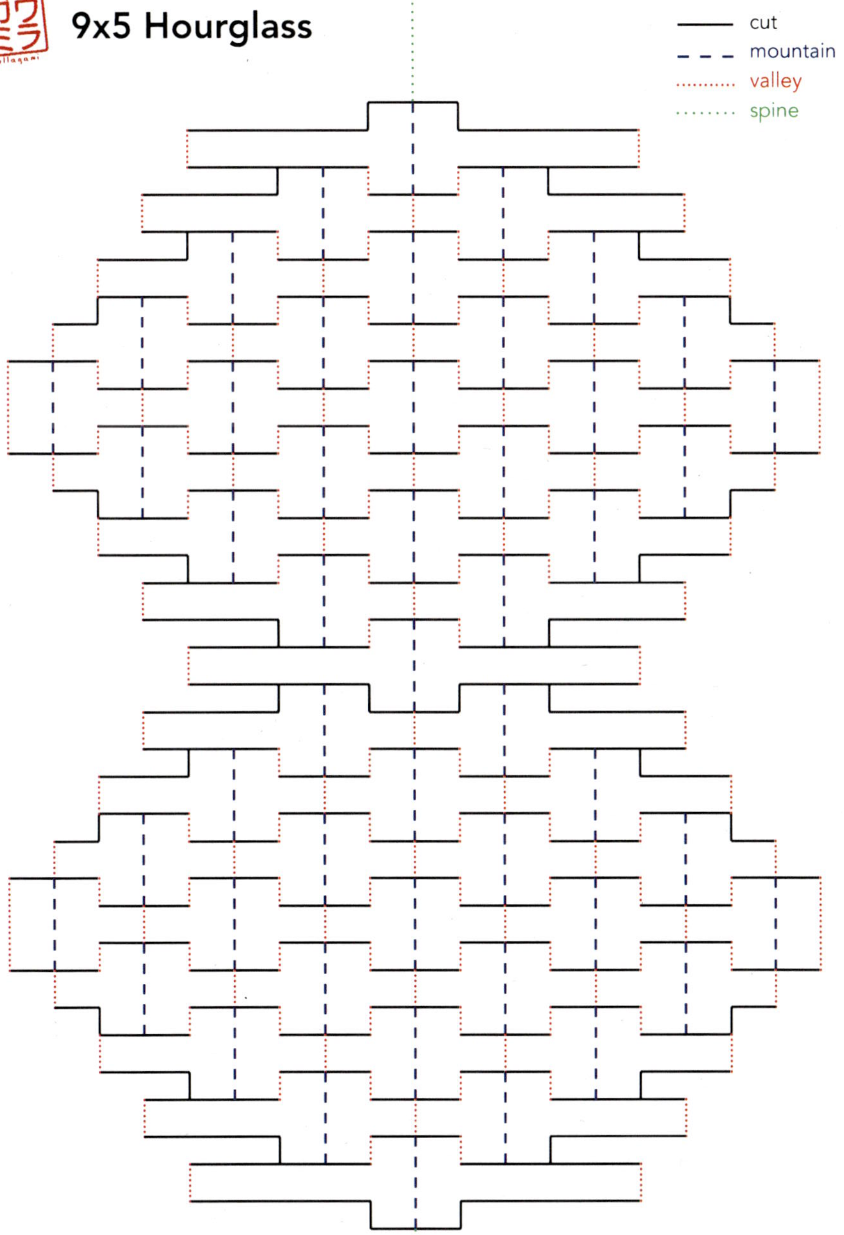

Conceived and designed by Guy Petzall ©2015. For more information, visit ullagami.com.

9x5 Hourglass

- cut
- mountain
- valley
- spine

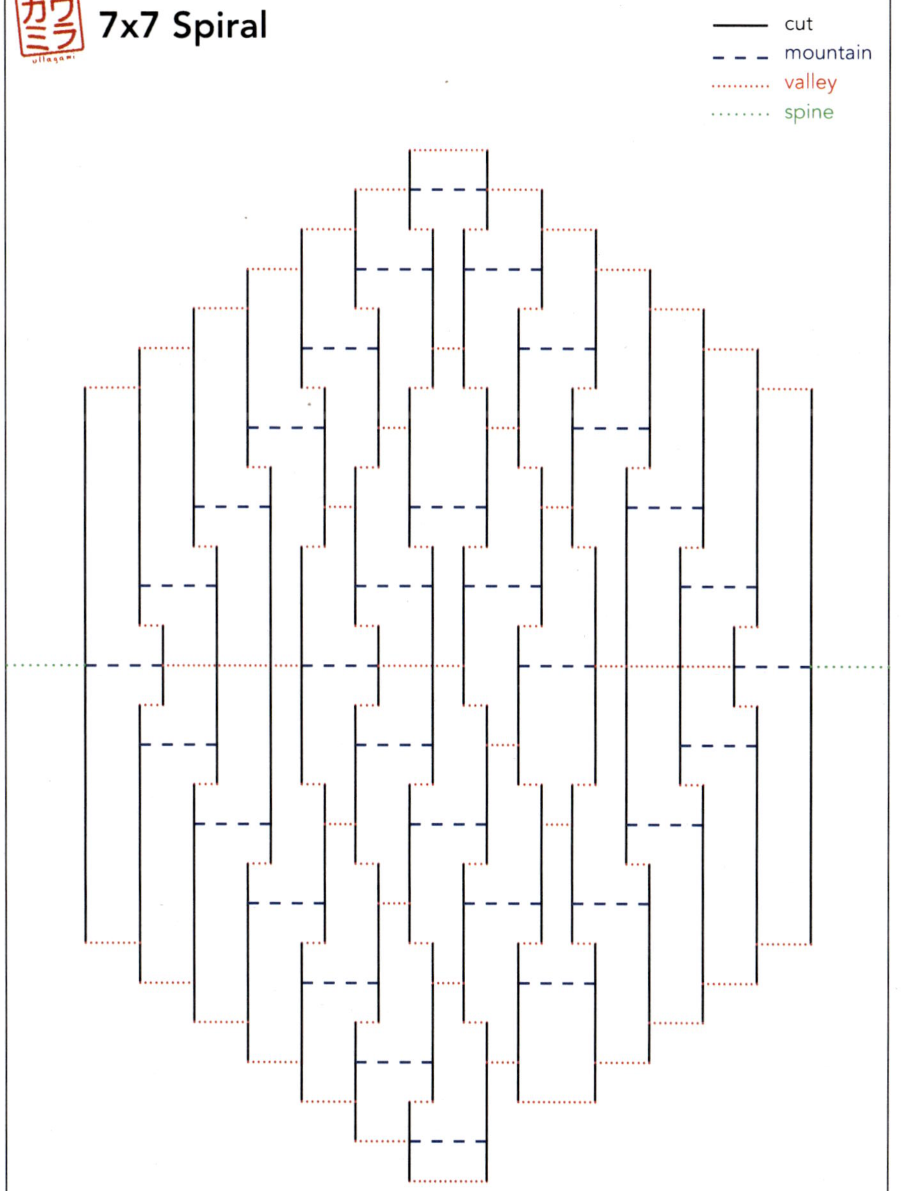

Conceived and designed by Guy Petzall ©2015. For more information, visit ullagami.com.

7x7 Eck Scross

Here's one from the Brutalist school of origamic architecture. And like a Brutalist building, there's something powerful and sturdy about it.

Mandala 1

A new departure, this model has lots of angled cuts. But it's the same folding principle as the 5x5 building blocks from which it's derived.

Just be careful to progress methodically, and not to miss any cuts.

7x7 Eck Scross

cut —
mountain – – –
valley ·····
spine ······

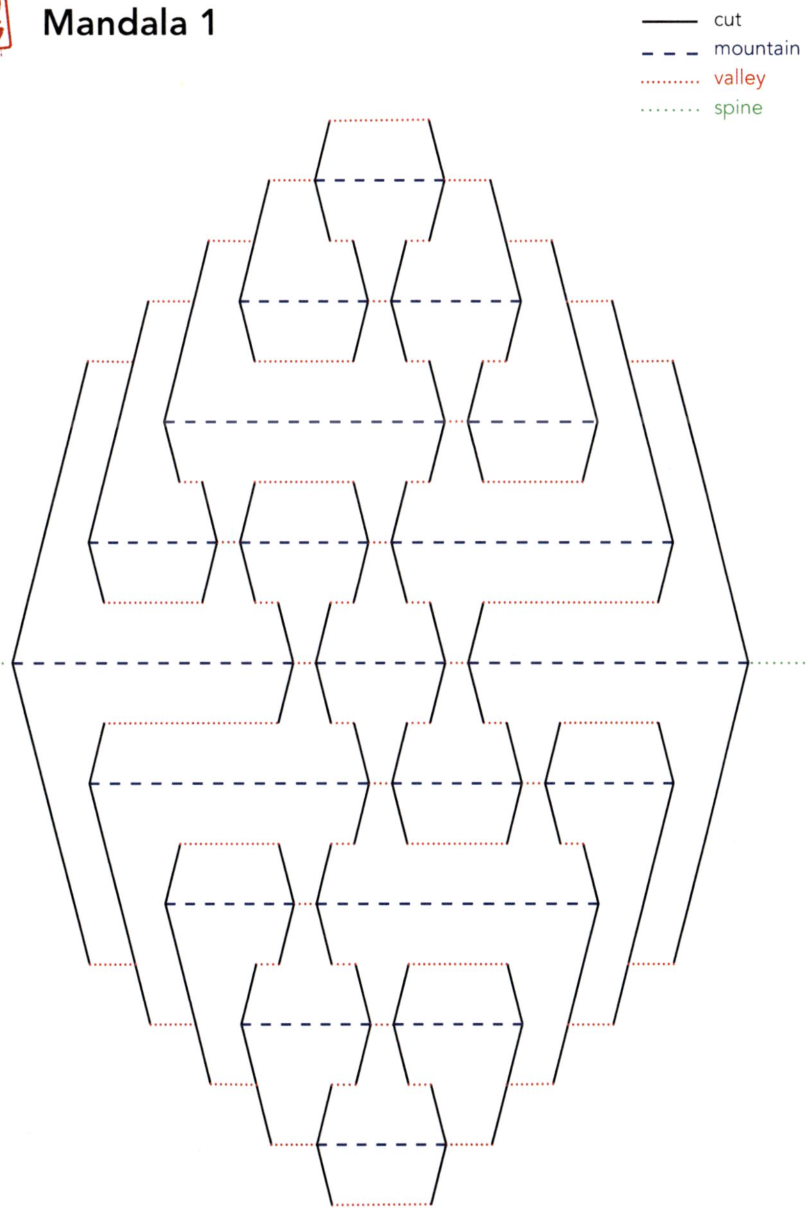

Conceived and designed by Guy Petzall ©2015. For more information, visit ullagami.com.

Mandala 1

cut —
mountain – – –
valley ·····
spine ······

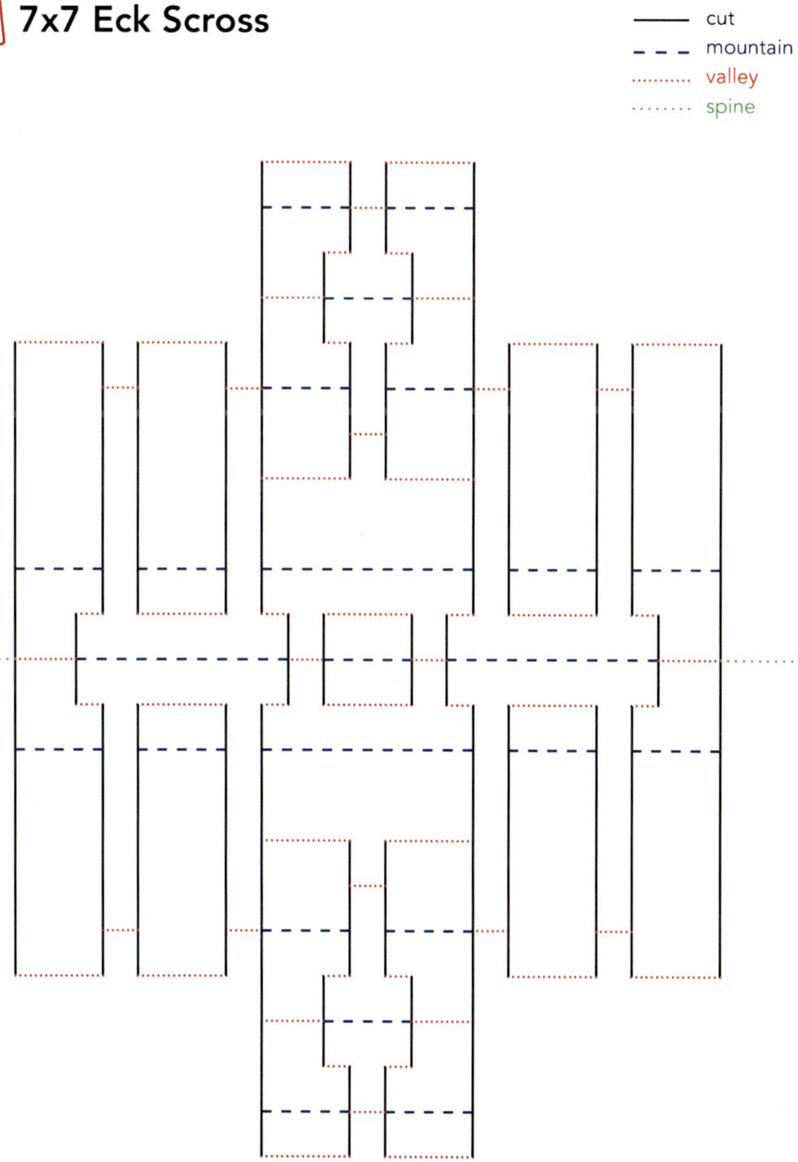

Conceived and designed by Guy Petzall ©2015. For more information, visit ullagami.com.

3x3 Obloid

The basic principle behind the obloid distortions is that all the varying dimensions – the shoulders, the necks, the faces – grow narrower toward the edges of the model. The result is a rounder, oval, aspect.

Also note that this is the first model whose spine is not exactly halfway down the page, because the model is taller than it is deep.

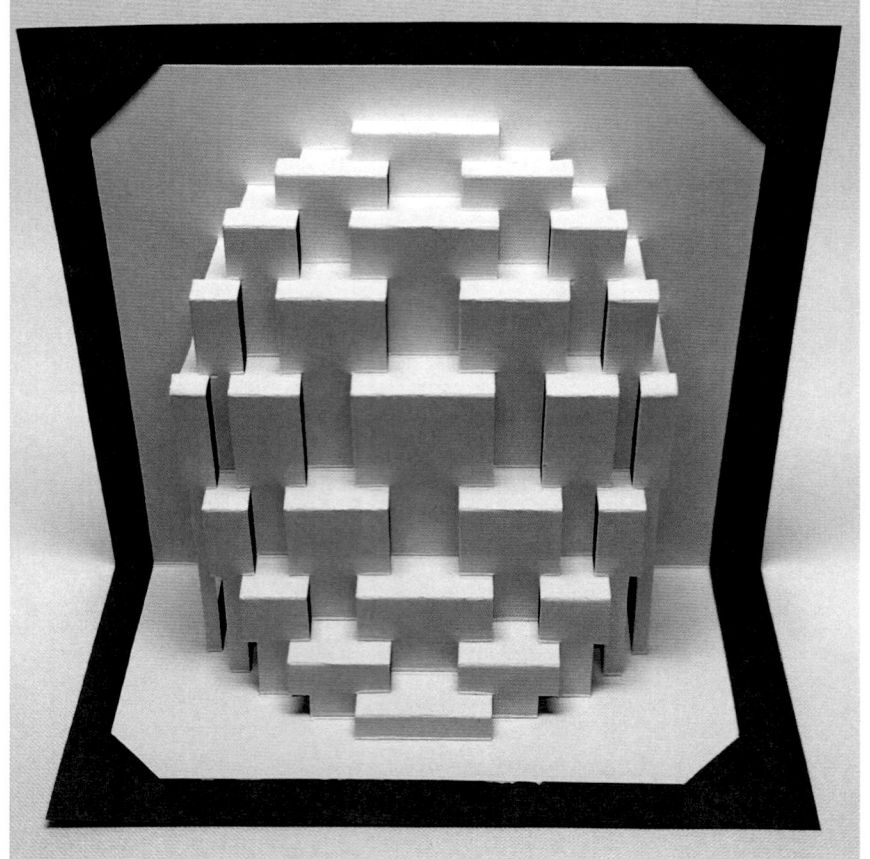

5x5 Obloid

Continuing the trend, but in greater detail. The new challenge here is the narrowness of the blocks' shoulders toward the left and right sides. Some very careful scoring and cutting is required, which is good practice for the models later in this book.

3x3 Obloid

— cut
-- mountain
··· valley
···· spine

5x5 Obloid

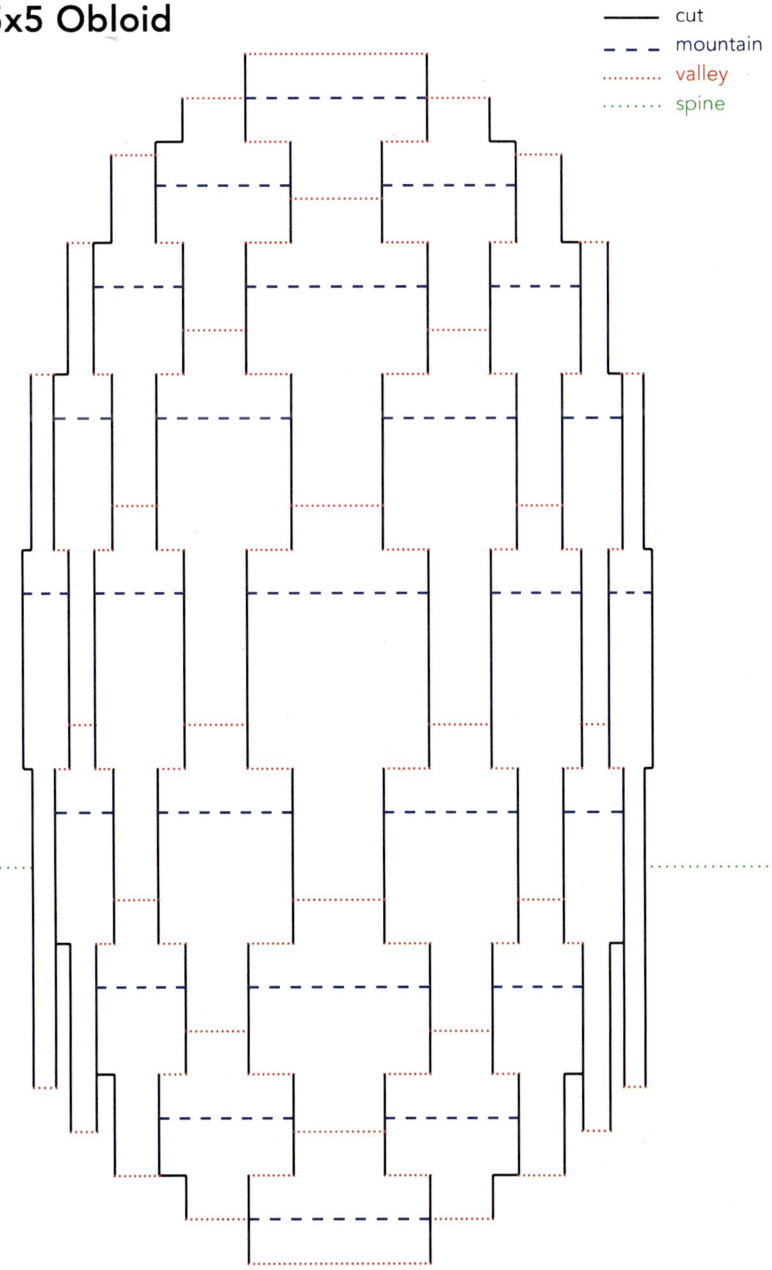

— cut
-- mountain
··· valley
···· spine

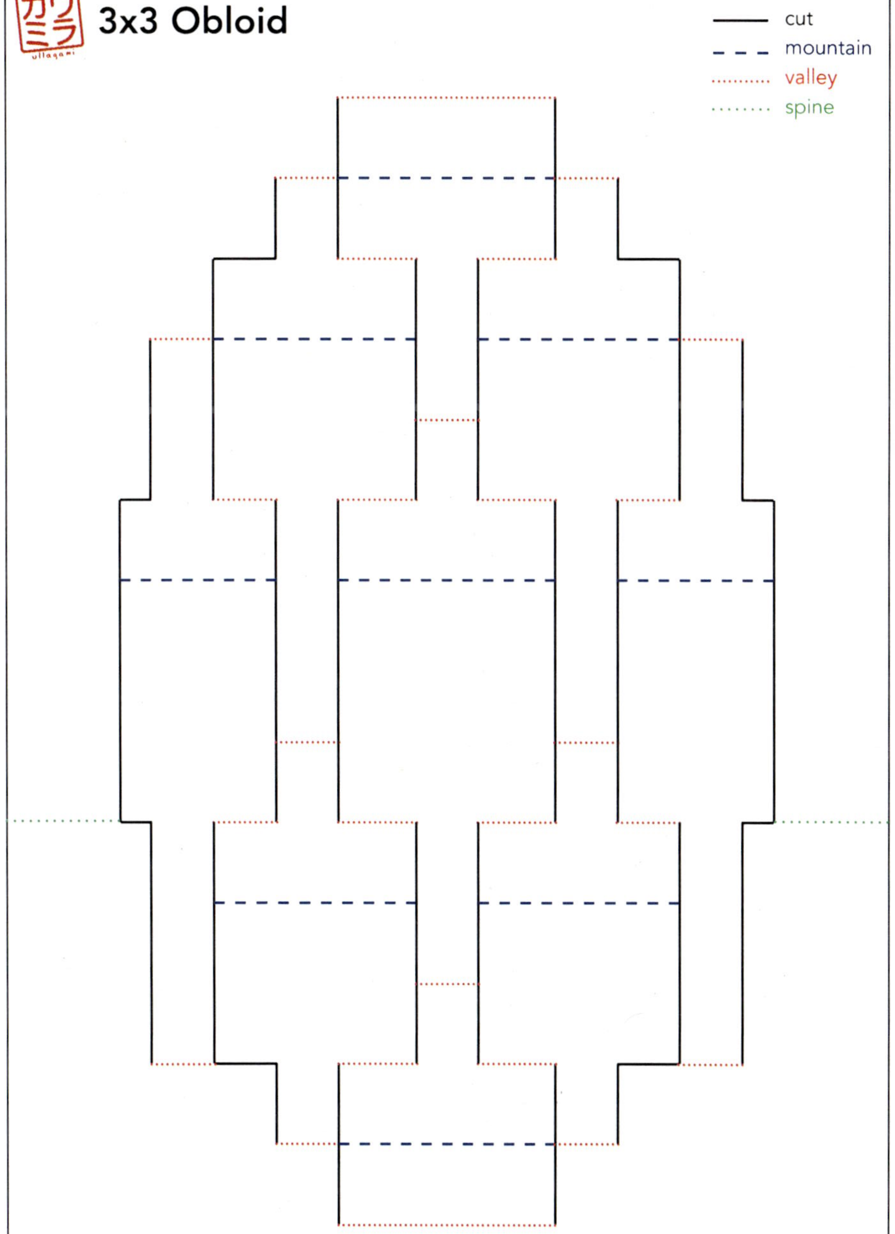

Conceived and designed by Guy Petzall ©2015. For more information, visit ullagami.com.

9x9 Diamond

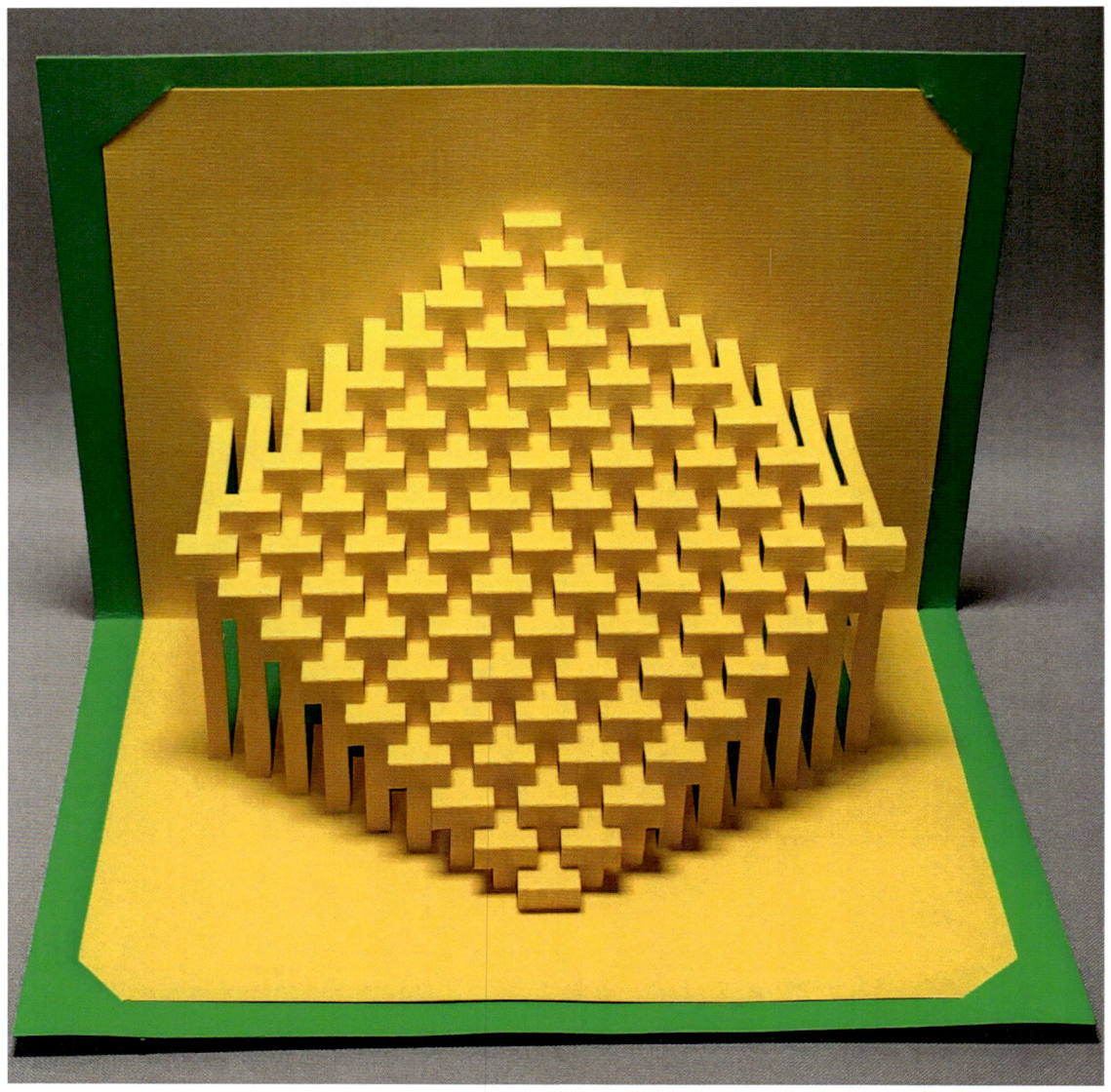

This is an obvious continuation of the models that have gone before: a simple diamond of regularly-spaced and -sized blocks. Of course we could further refine the pattern, expanding to ever more blocks, but 9x9 is a good balance point for two reasons: the more blocks we have, the smaller they must be to fit on a single page; and there are many interesting patterns which you can make using this basic 9x9 grid as a starting point.

This and all the diamond patterns to follow fold exactly in half, and the blocks themselves collapse to the same line. What this means in terms of practicality is that the final model, when collapsed flat, is quite thick where all the blocks pile up. It's therefore a good idea to use a thinner cardstock for these models, especially considering that they are generally quite structurally robust without the need for heavier card.

9x9 Diamond ZigZag

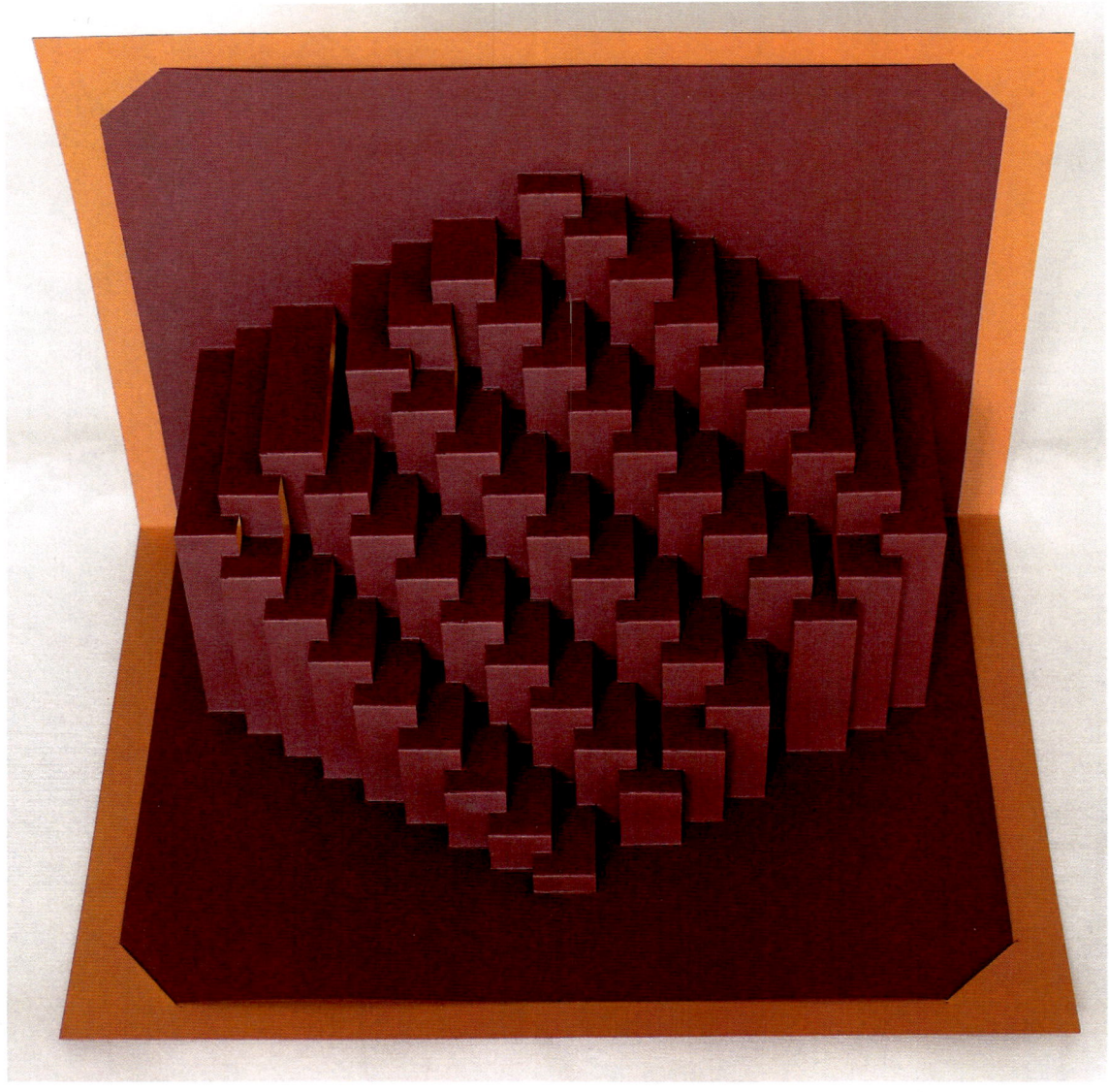

Our first pattern created by supressing blocks from the grid. That is, a number of blocks have been "removed" from the basic diamond grid, revealing a zig-zag of remaining blocks.

Here is a diagram of which blocks have stayed and which have been suppressed. It's a regular progression, resulting in a model which looks almost like a stairway, with 49 steps from the bottom to the top.

You can also see that the "arms" and "legs" are not notched as in the previous model. Purely as a matter of taste, certain models benefit from this more sturdy appearance.

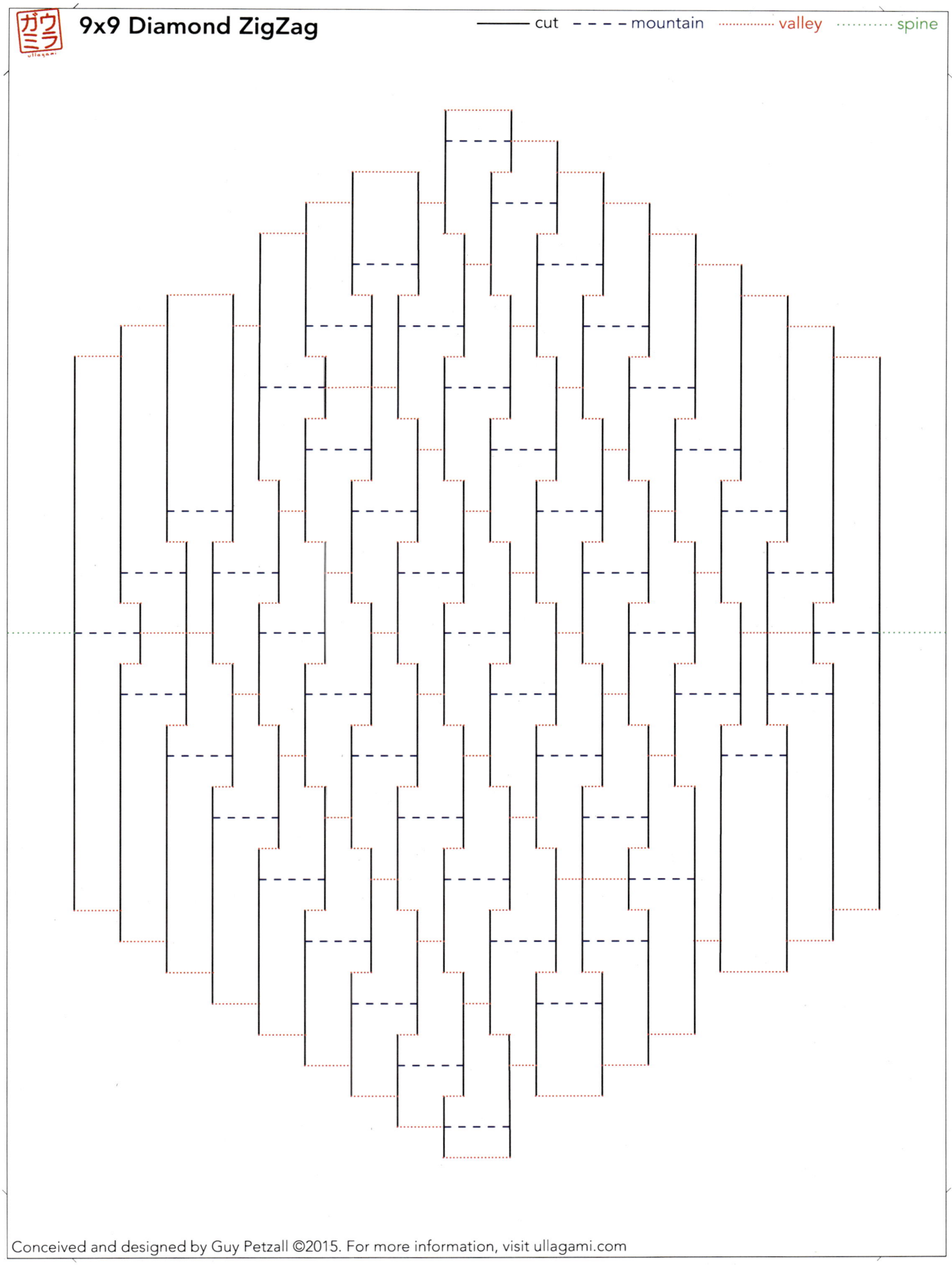

9x9 Diamond Spiral

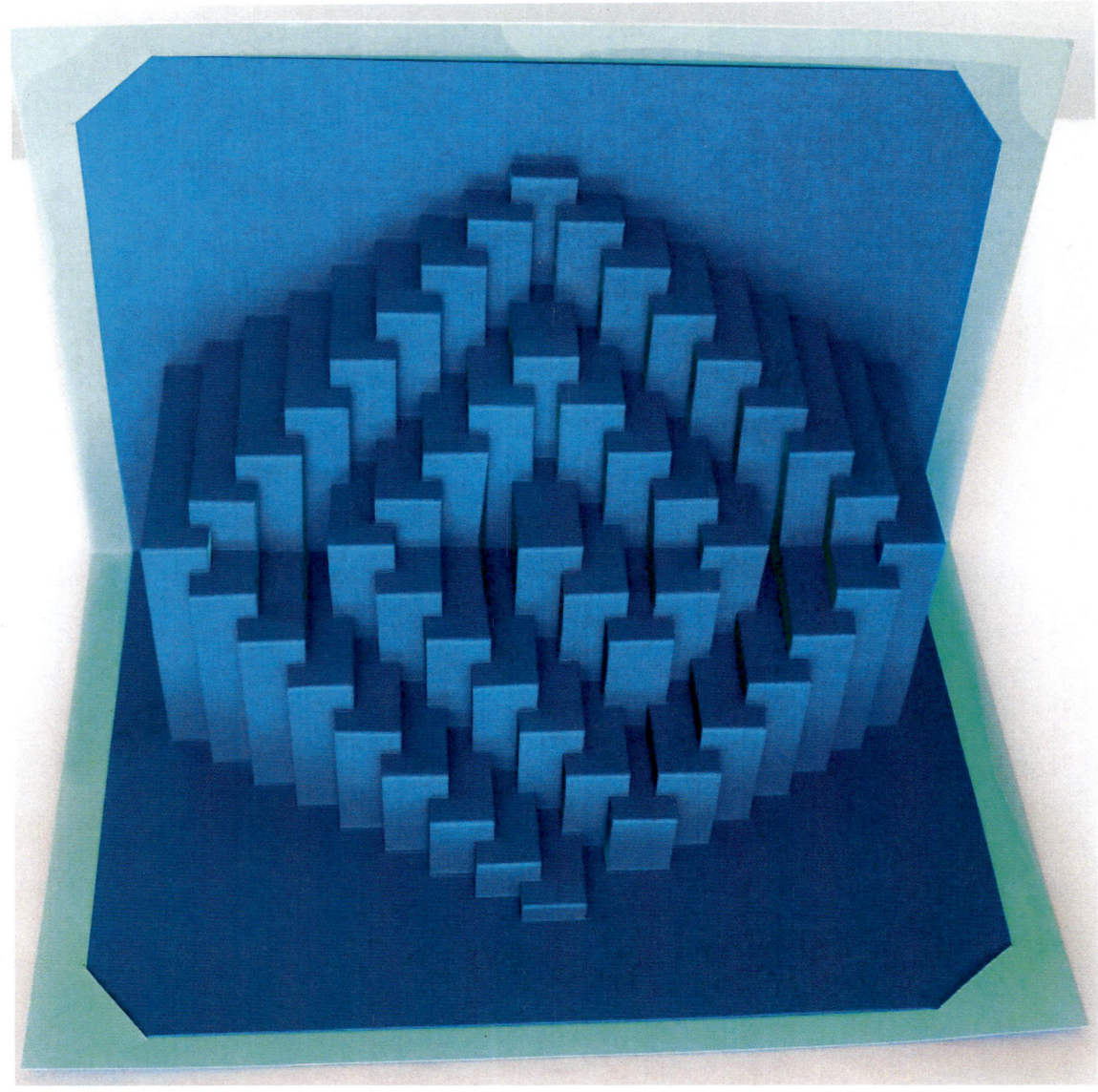

There are $2^{81}-1$, which is 2,417,851,639,229,258,349,412,351 different patterns we can make in this way, but the regular ones look the best.

Here is a spiral pattern, starting at the bottom block and winding clockwise to the center. Again it makes a 49-step stairway.

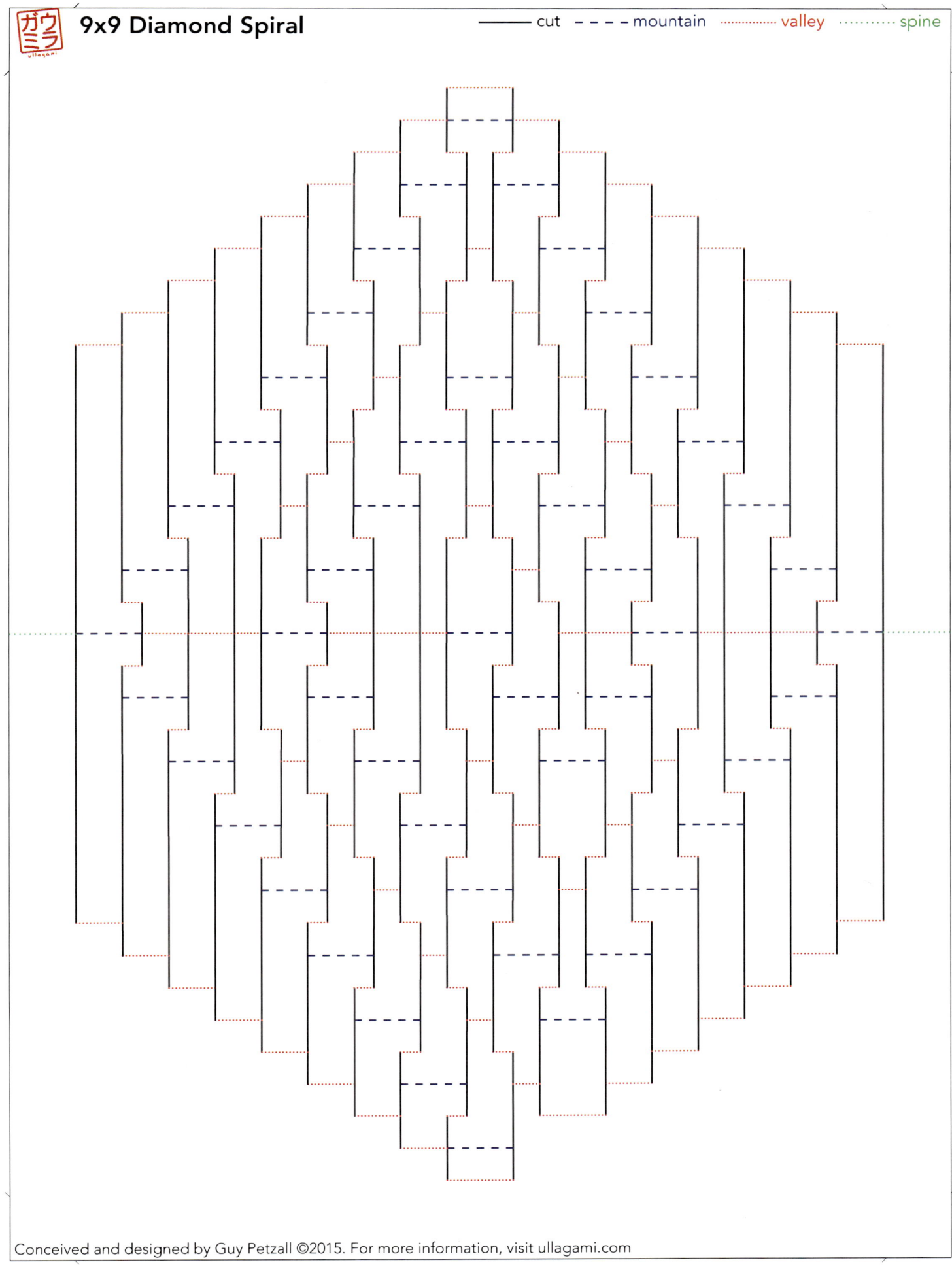

9x9 Vertical Meander

The meander is an ancient Greek tiling motif. It was frequently used as a mosaic border, with many meanders all linked together. We will do that too, later in this book; but even as a single non-repeating unit of this pattern, it's quite a pretty model, that forces your eyes to follow its swirl of shadows.

Again, 49 blocks remain.

9x9 Vertical Meander

— cut --- mountain ······ valley ······ spine

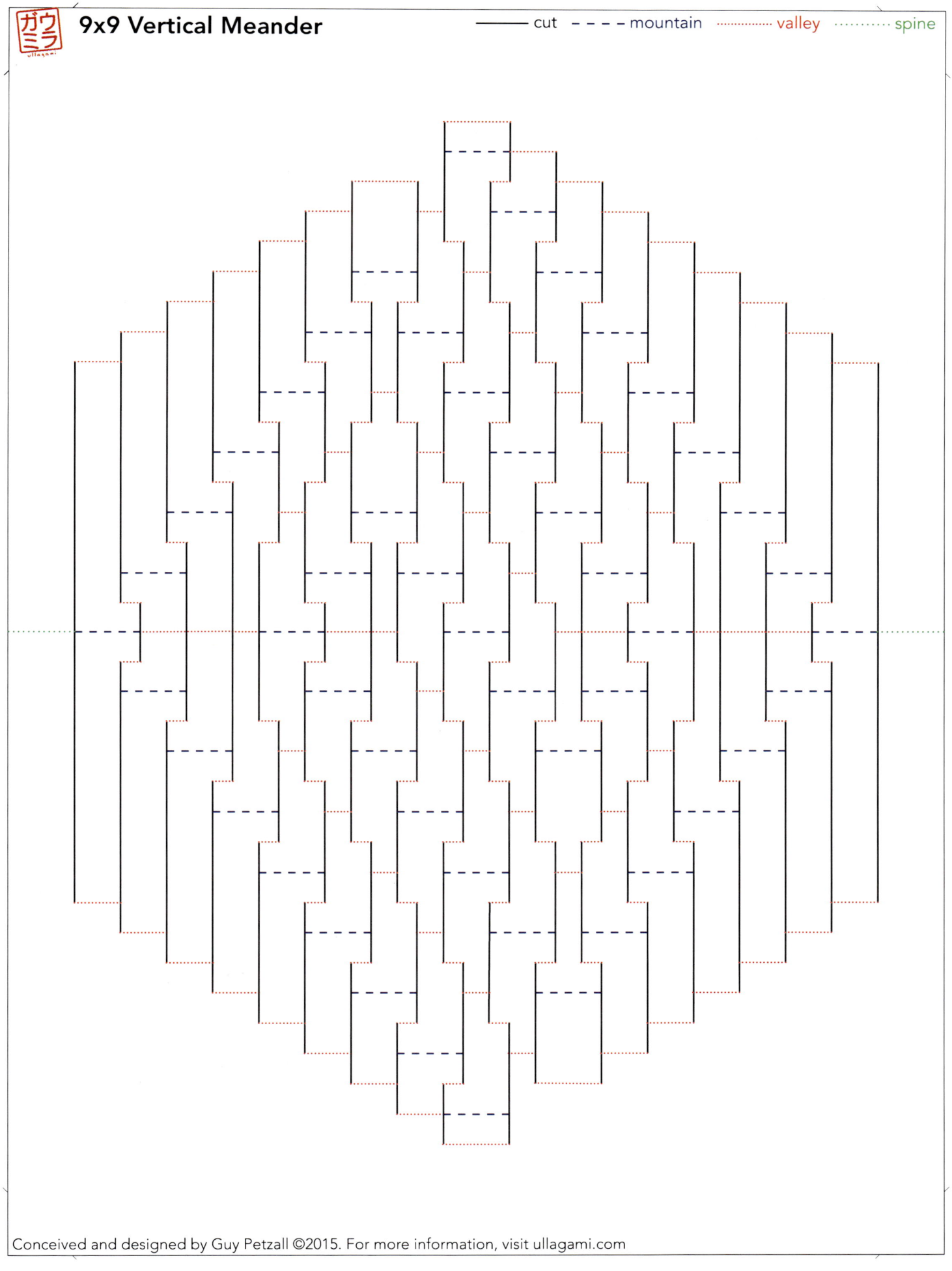

Conceived and designed by Guy Petzall ©2015. For more information, visit ullagami.com

9x9 Meander 2

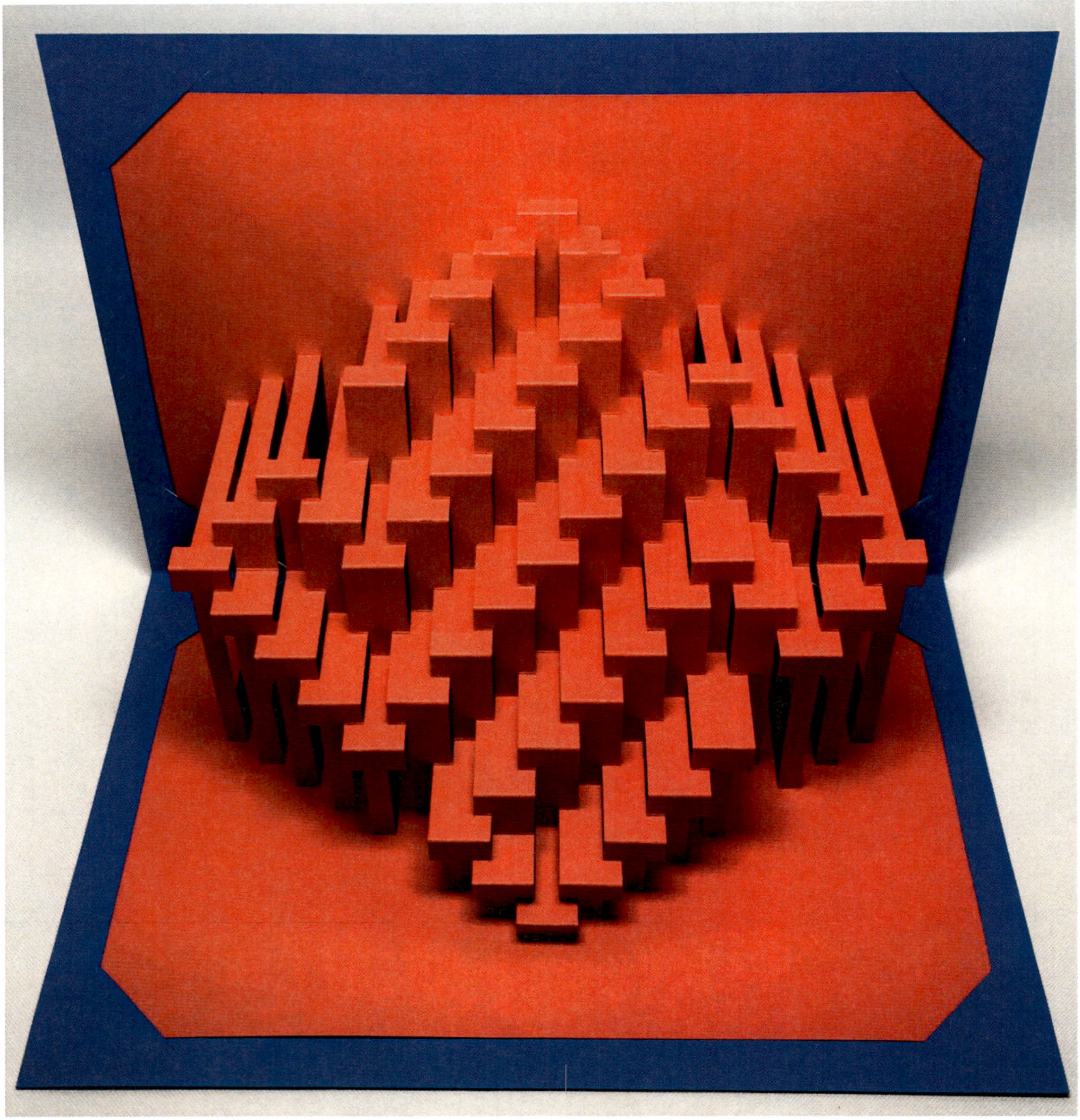

A variation on the meander pattern, this one begins and ends in the middle of opposite sides, rather than at the corners.

The notched descenders have been reintroduced, because it somehow just looks better with this pattern.

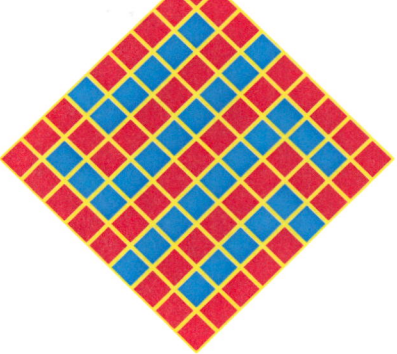

Split Quarters

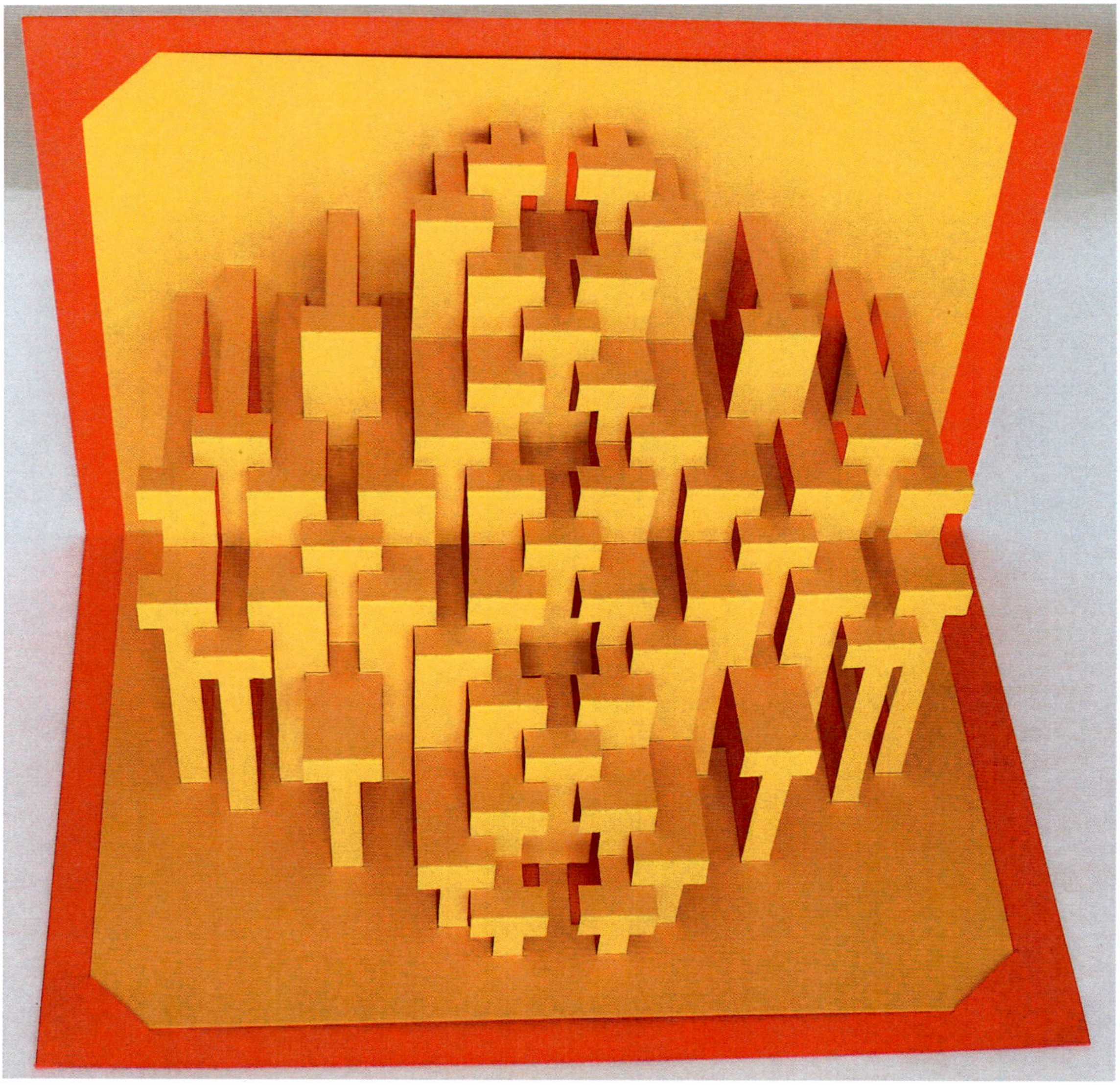

So many patterns hidden within the grid. The idea of this one began as an excercise in dividing and then sub-dividing the available space. The result is quite spiky-looking, maybe a little crazed, but still entirely regular and symmetrical.

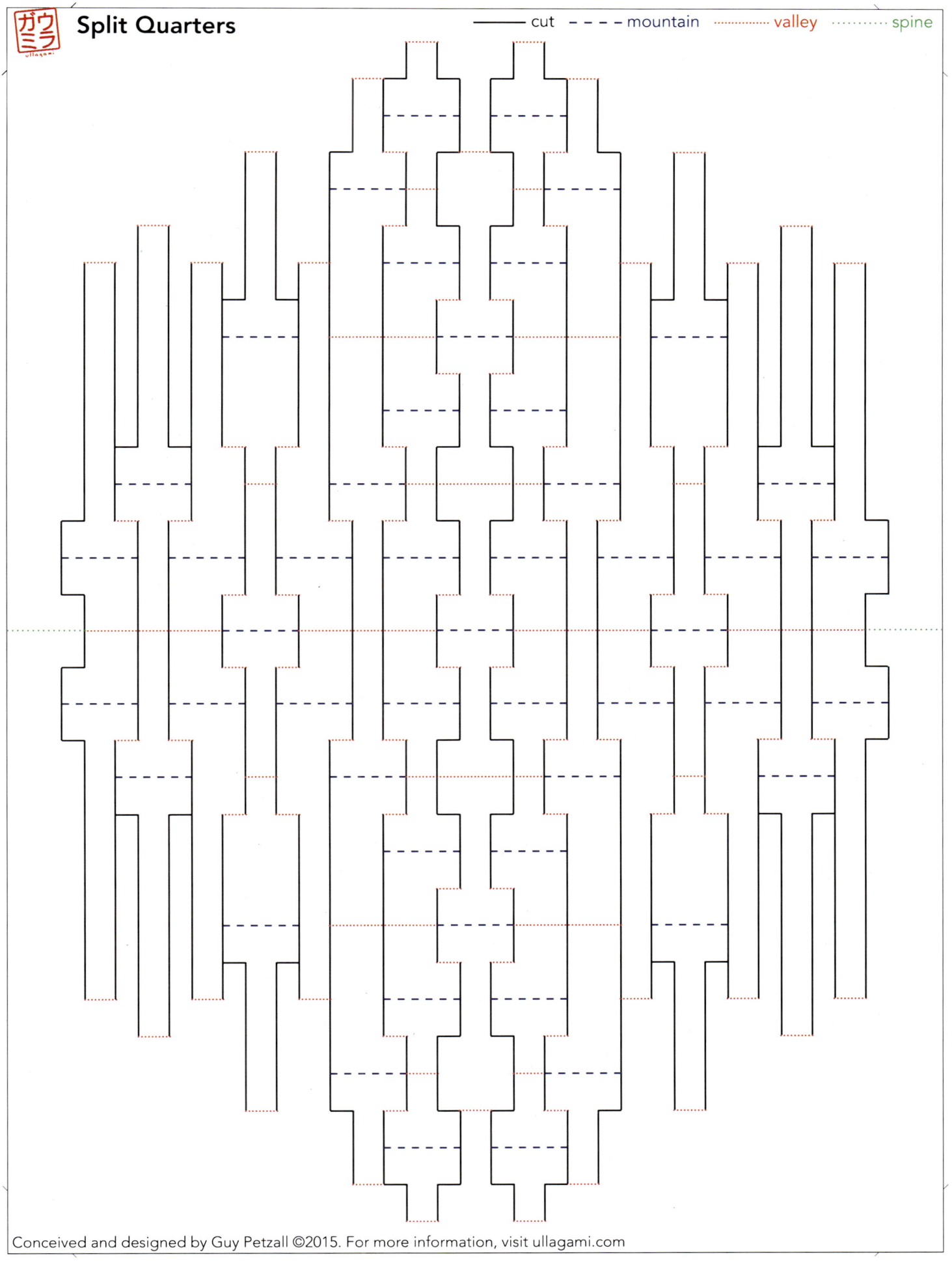

Obloid

This model, inspired by Vasarely, is what happens when you apply some math to an existing design. Structurally, this model is identical to the 9x9 Diamond we've already seen. But here, the model has been distorted in 3 ways: the width of the blocks, the space between the blocks, and their heights have all undergone transformation toward the center block, and the result is a much rounder final shape where we had a straight-edged diamond before.

Obloid

— cut --- mountain ···· valley ···· spine

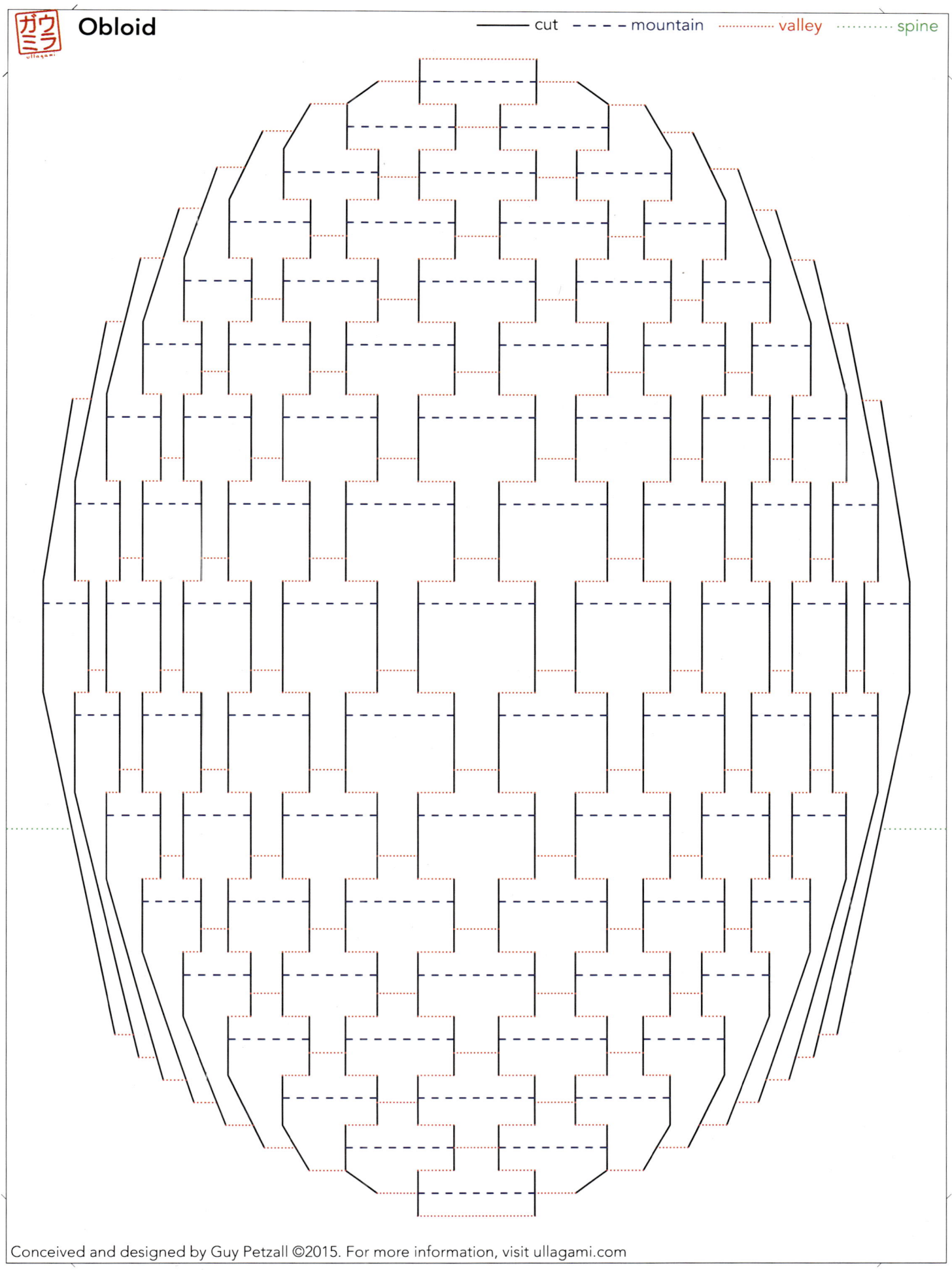

Conceived and designed by Guy Petzall ©2015. For more information, visit ullagami.com

Obloid ZigZag

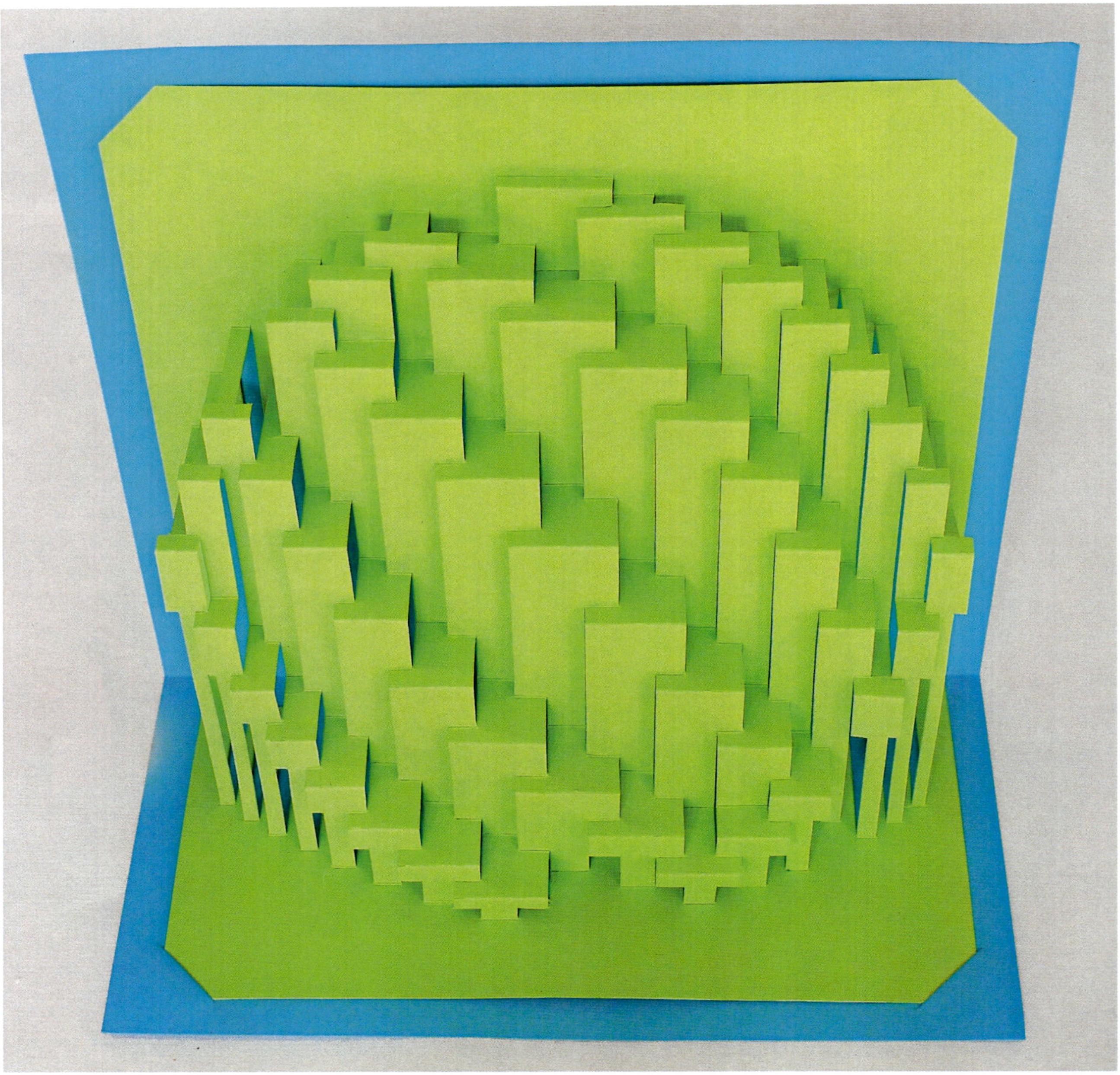

... and with a new kind of 9x9 space to play with, we can revisit some of the same motfis we cut into the original diamond grid. Here is the ZigZag, reinvented round.

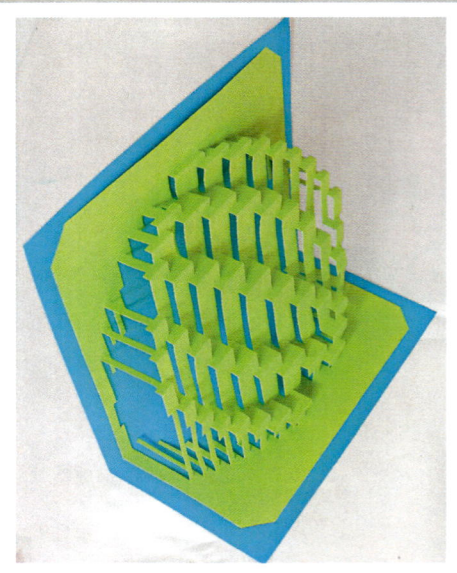

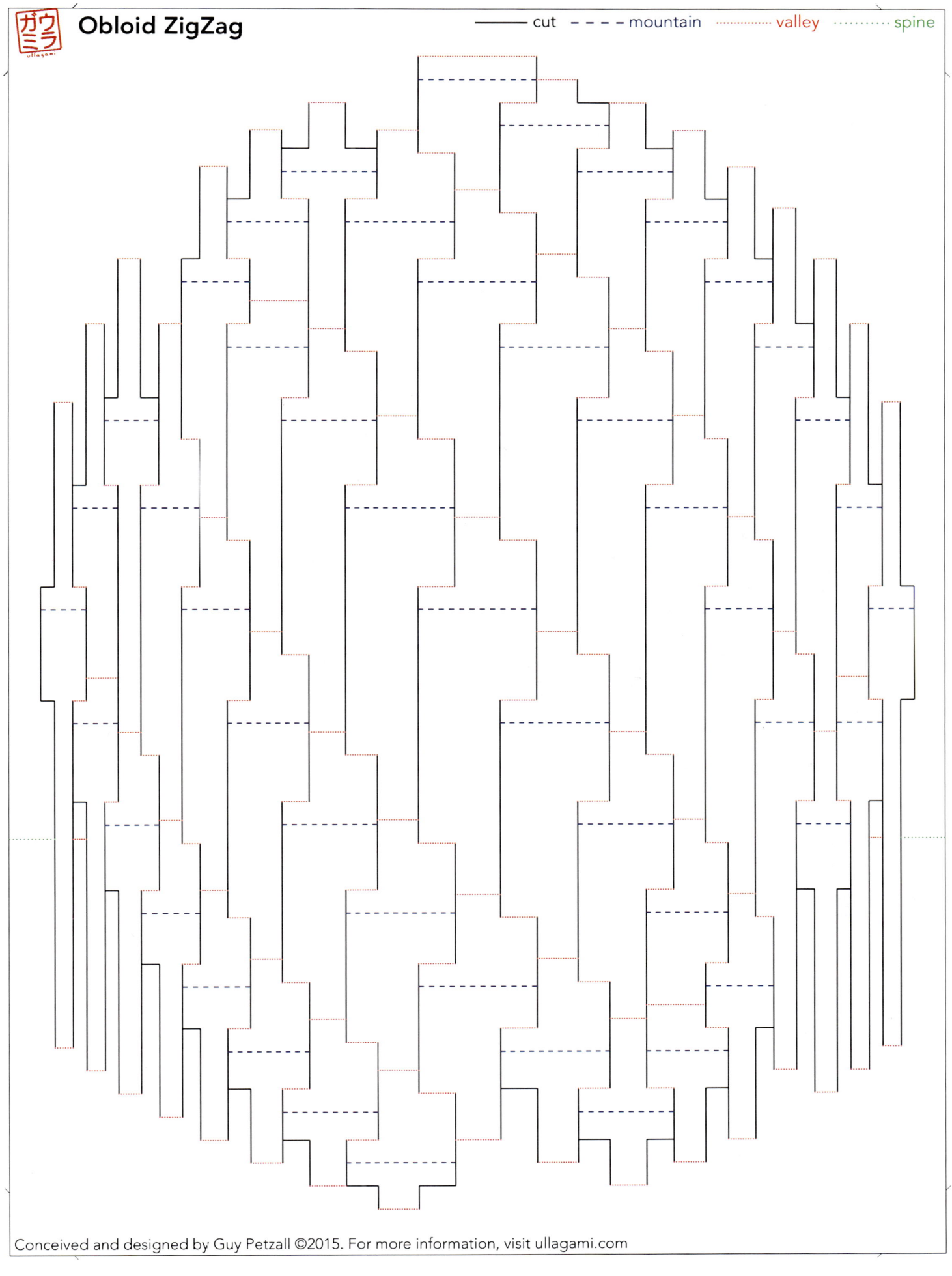

Obloid Spiral

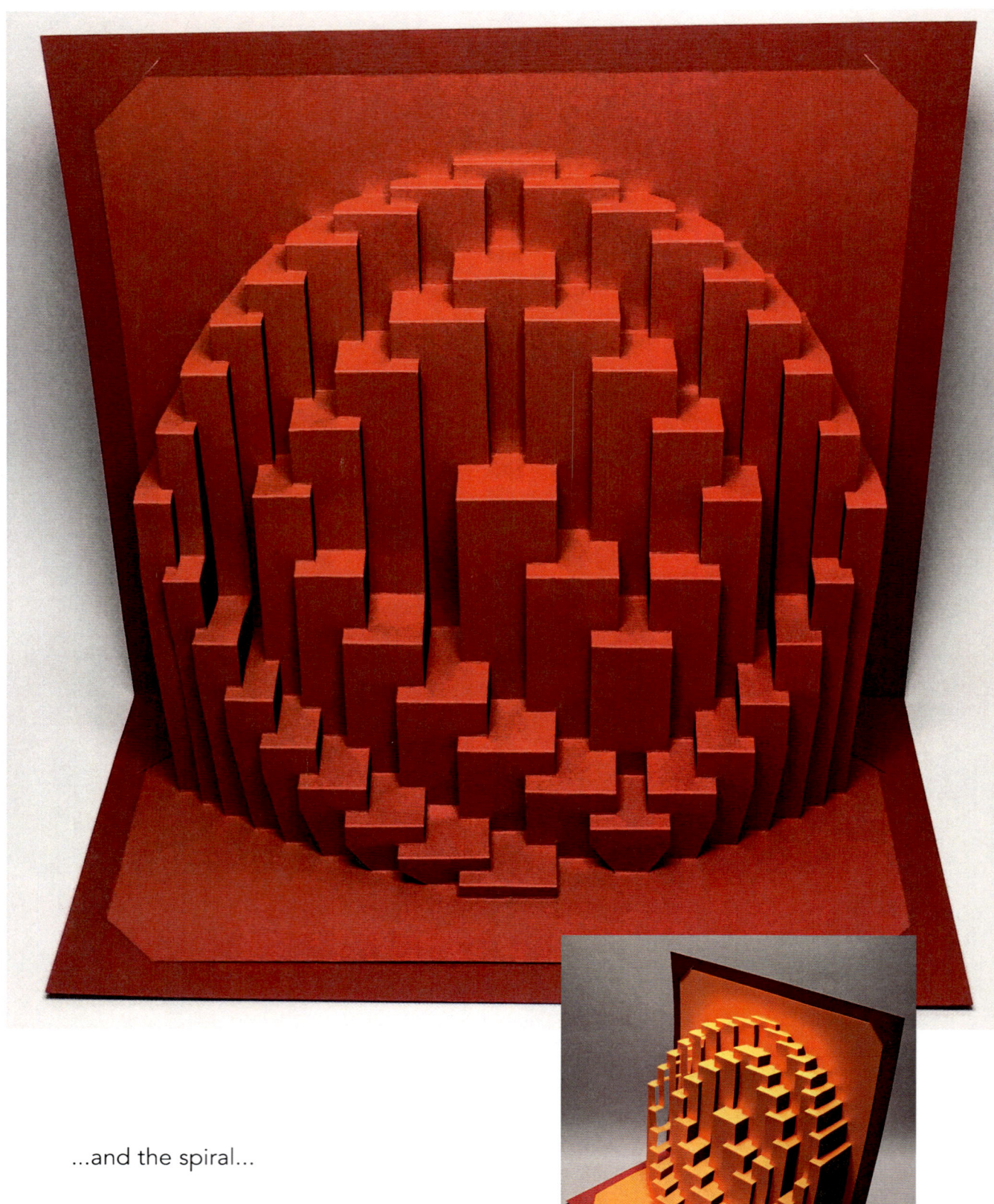

...and the spiral...

40

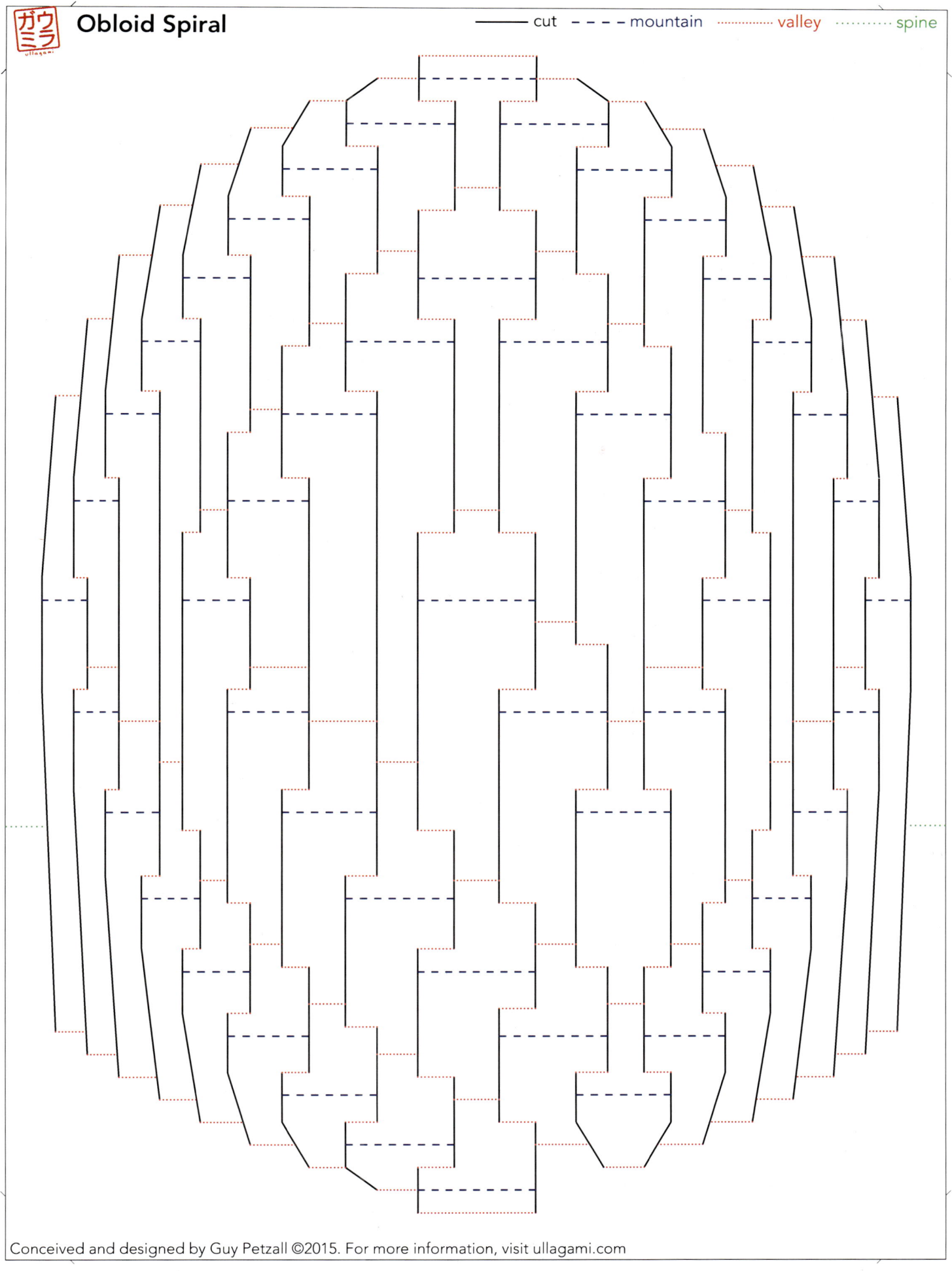

Obloid Whorl

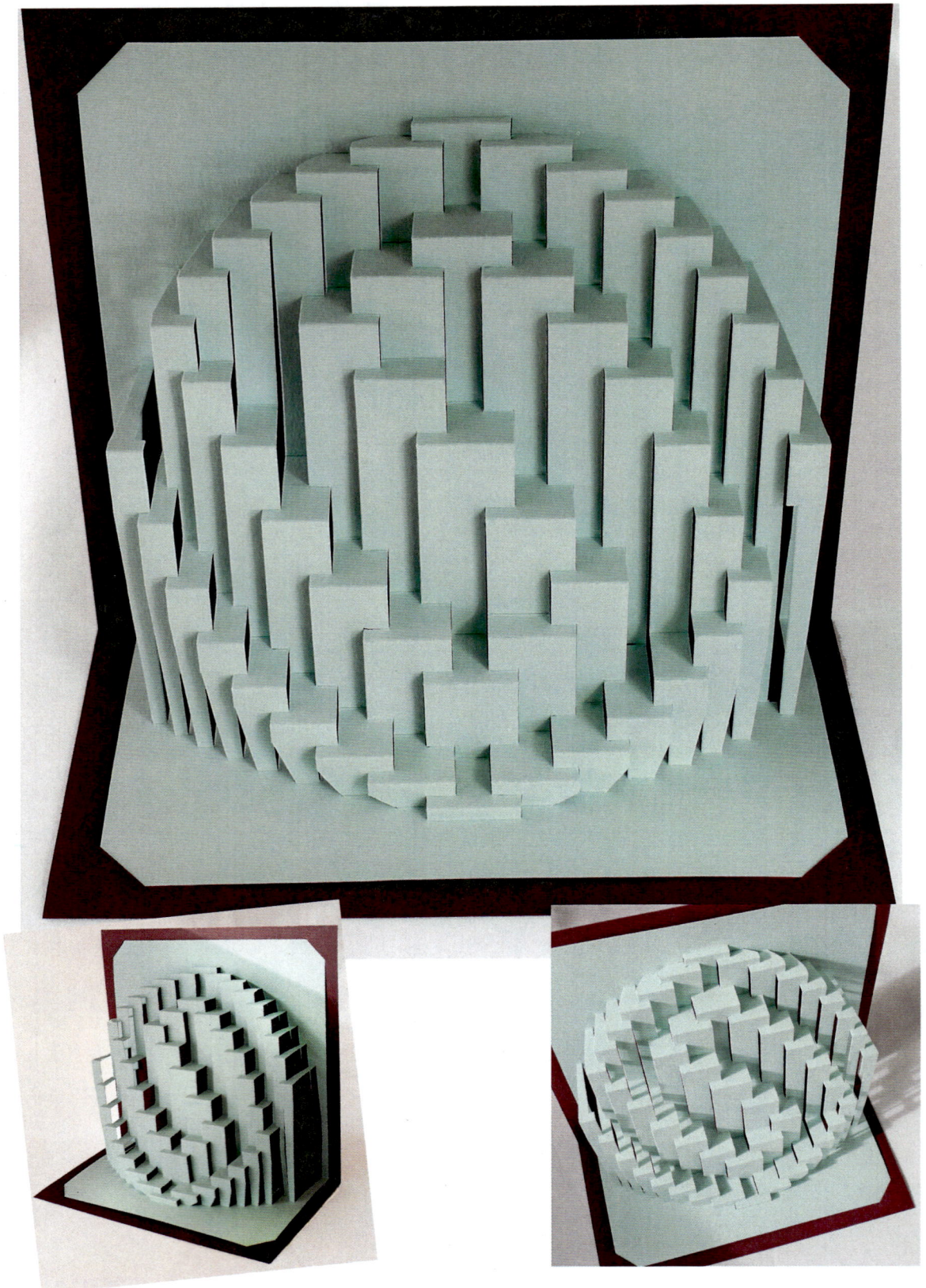

You might recognize this pattern. It's the Meander motif, reinvented in Obloid space. But once presented in this softer, rounder way, it loses its rigid-Greek-mosaic-pattern aspect, and looks more like a swirling galaxy. And so the name "Whorl" seems to fit it better.

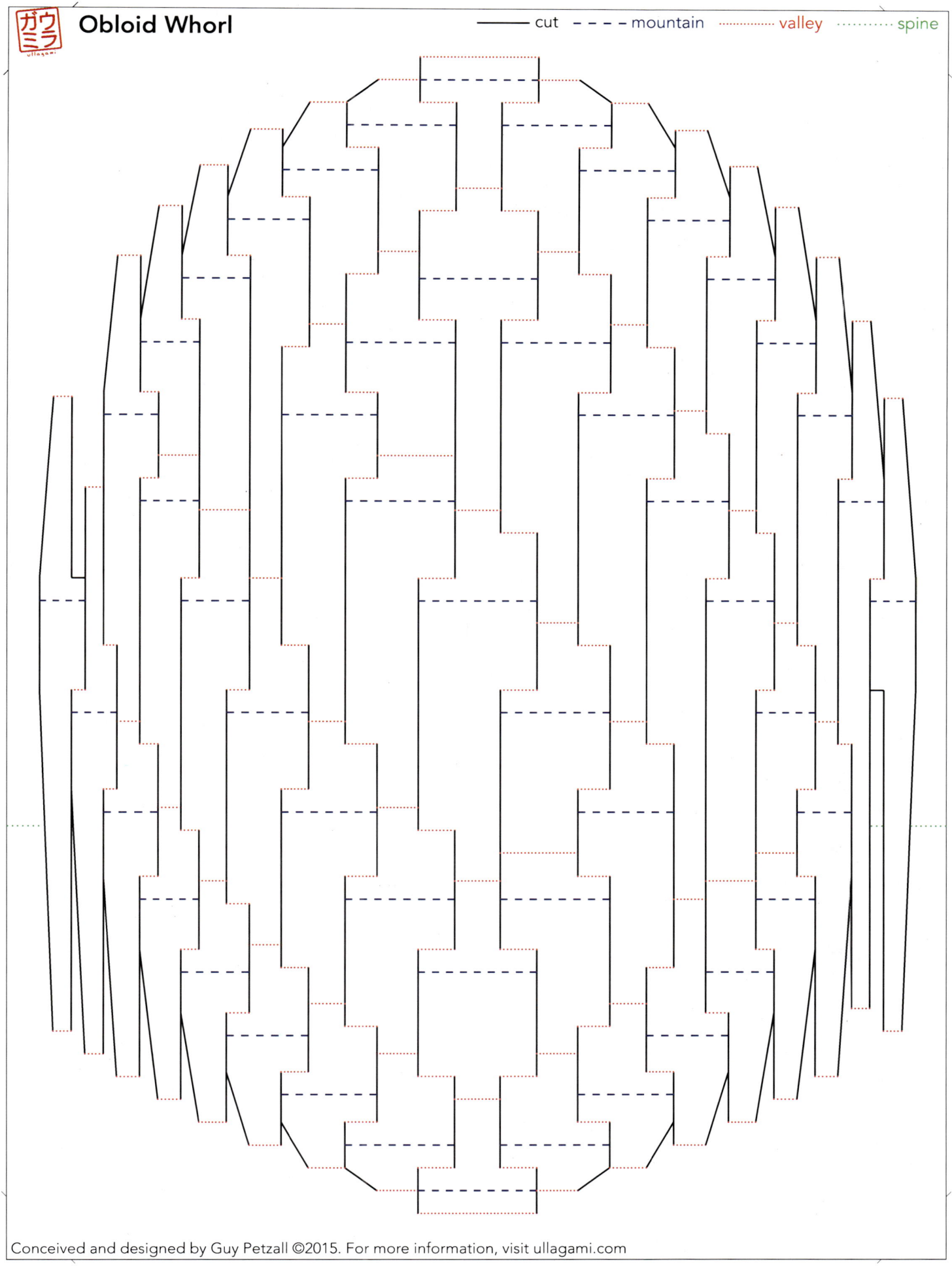

Linked Meanders

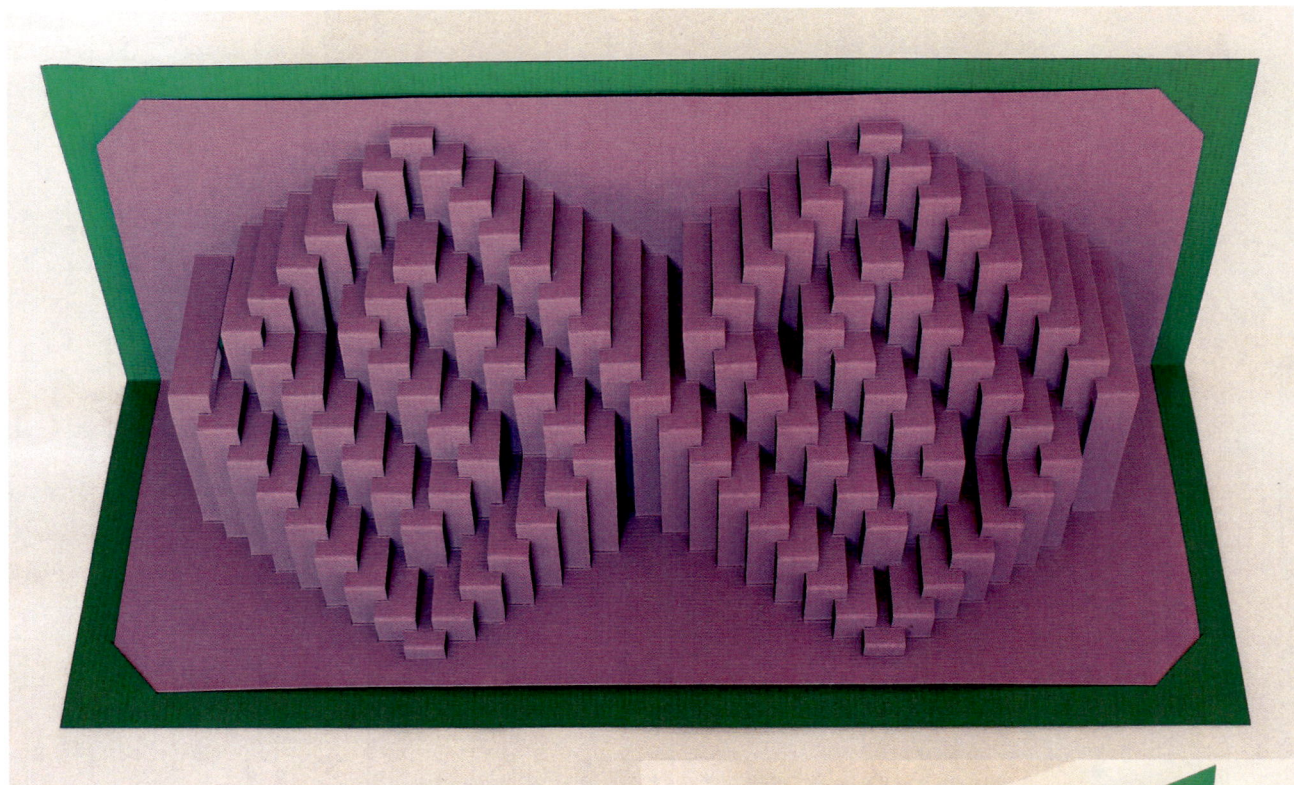

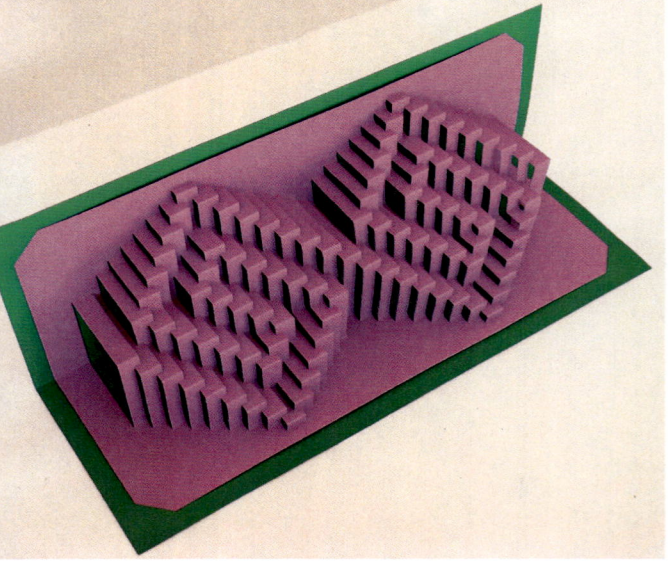

Here are two 9x9 Diamond Meanders, linked together. They're a little different from the stand-alone version, notably the whole motif has been rotated 90° to make the endpoints coincide. And because it's double-wide, the page has been rotated to accomodate. The scale is slightly closer and tighter than the original, which gives the finished model a nice sense of complexity while being only a little bit harder to fold.

Linked Meanders

— cut - - - mountain .... valley .... spine

Conceived and designed by Guy Petzall ©2015. For more information, visit ullagami.com

Knight Moves

Here we have something of a departure from what has gone before.

This model's design began as a chess-board-like grid, over which is laid a regular pattern of knight's moves, which made for an offset – but nonetheless regular – grid-within-a-grid.

And then, to bring the grid of moves into a more pleasing alignment, the whole design was skewed 30° and trimmed to fit the dimensions of the paper.

The result is an off-kilter array of slanting shards, as the mounted chessman hops his way around the page.

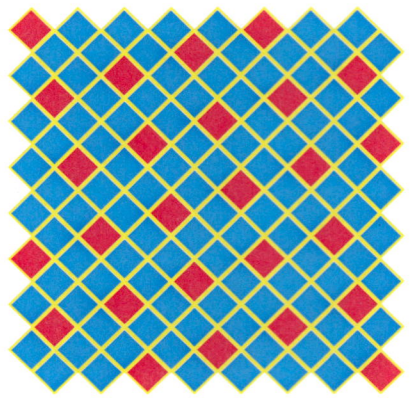

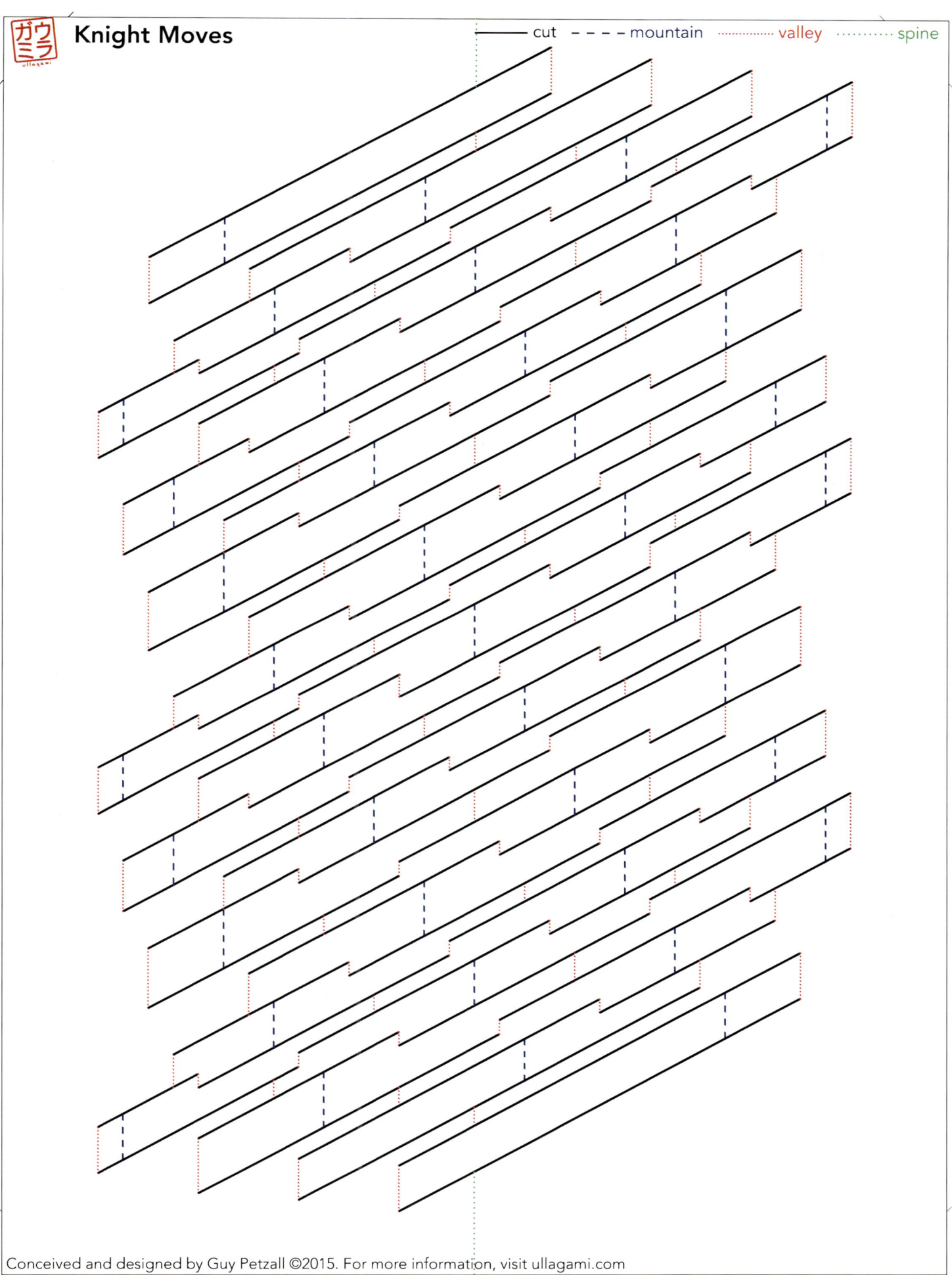

Wavey

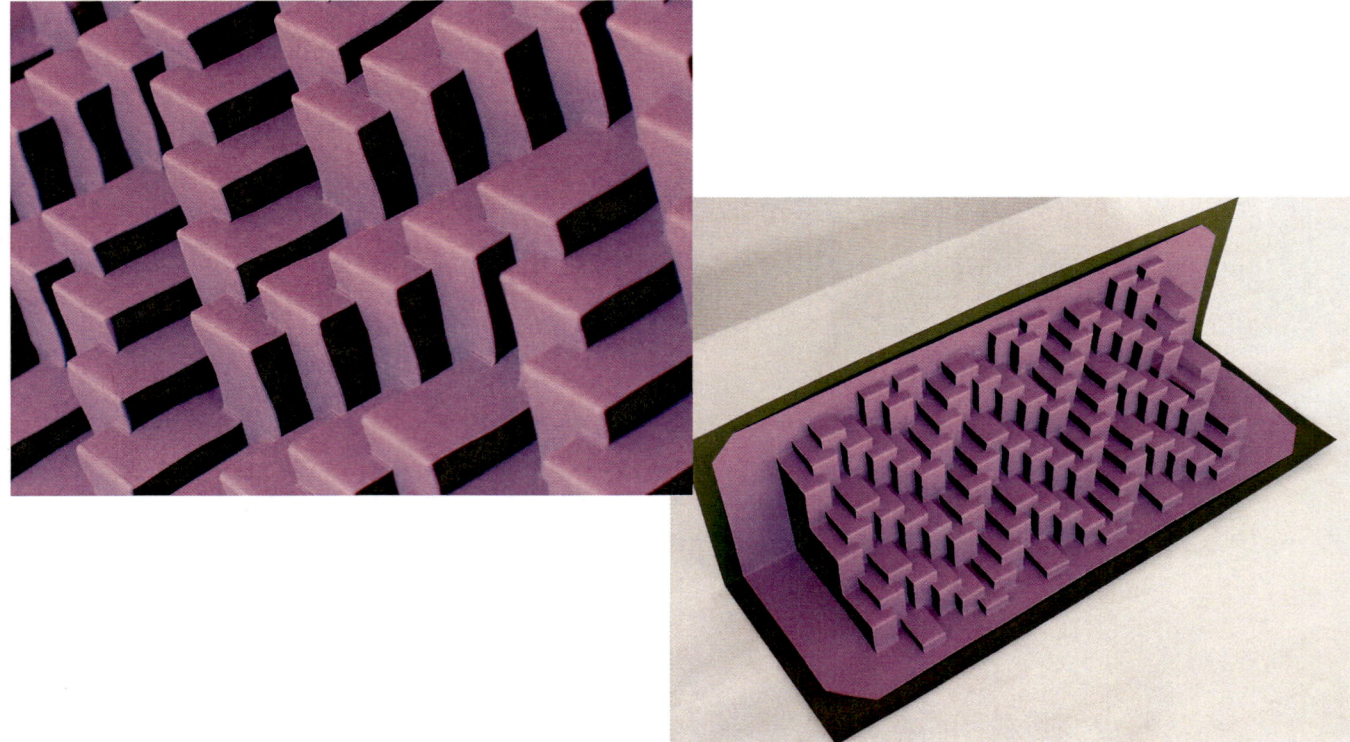

A continuation of a theme: expanding patterns to fill the paper. Here is a sine wave/zigzag construction. Pattern-wise it's simple enough, but the construction still requires some dexterity to get perfect.

For the centermost areas, it is important to work from both sides of the paper, and because of the paucity of surrounding background surface, you should consider slightly heavier card for this project, to improve the model's self-supporting structure.

Wavey

— cut --- mountain ⋯ valley ⋯ spine

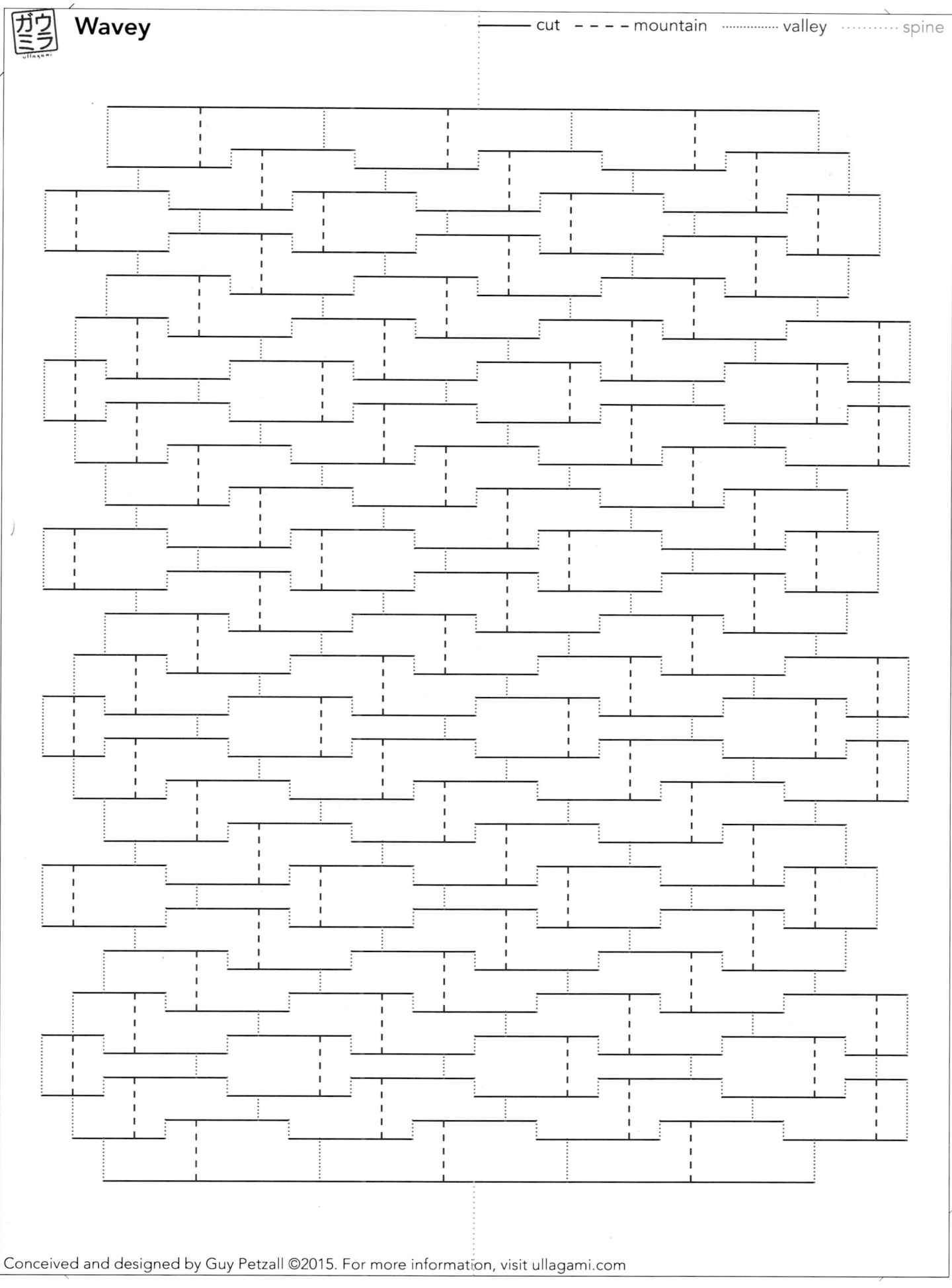

Conceived and designed by Guy Petzall ©2015. For more information, visit ullagami.com

Meandered Spirals

Sometimes simple is beautiful.

This model isn't particularly complex or difficult to construct, but it is nonetheless handsome.

The pattern concept is the marriage of two 5x5 spirals, connected by a 5x5 meander.

Speaking of marriage, I once made one of these for a fellow who

wanted to give it as an anniversary present to his wife. Before he presented it to her, he composed a poem of a structure corresponding to this model. One word of the poem was written on each block's top and face, and it was written such that his wife could read either the even-numbered lines (on the tops of the blocks), or the odd-numbered lines (on the faces of the blocks) or all the lines together, and have a different complete poem each time. It was a beautiful complement to the original cutting, and a very thoughtful gift.

Spiralink

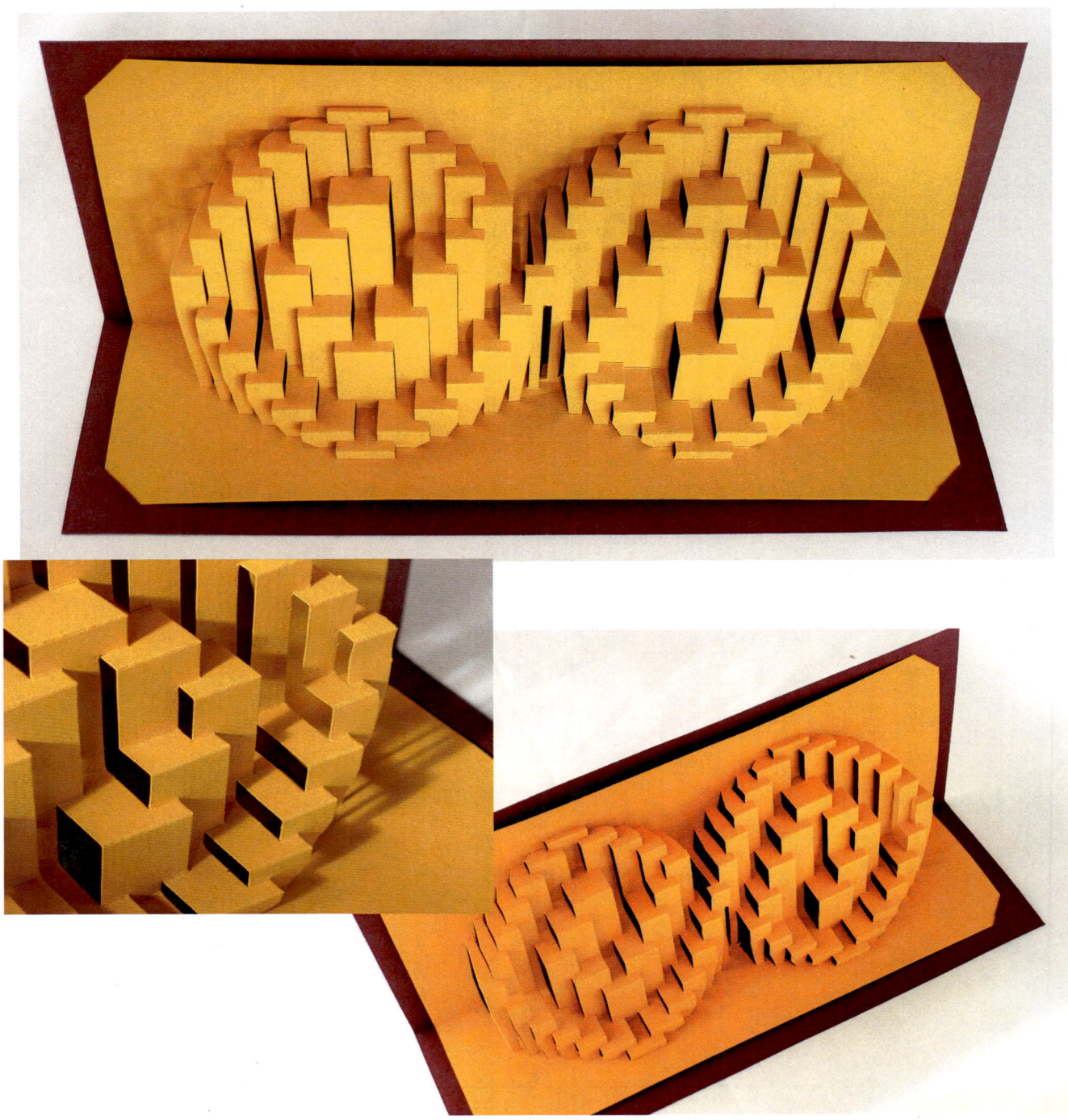

Again two linked spirals, but this time with Obloid shapes. The result is a much rounder, softer look, even though it's still composed entirely of straight folds and cuts.

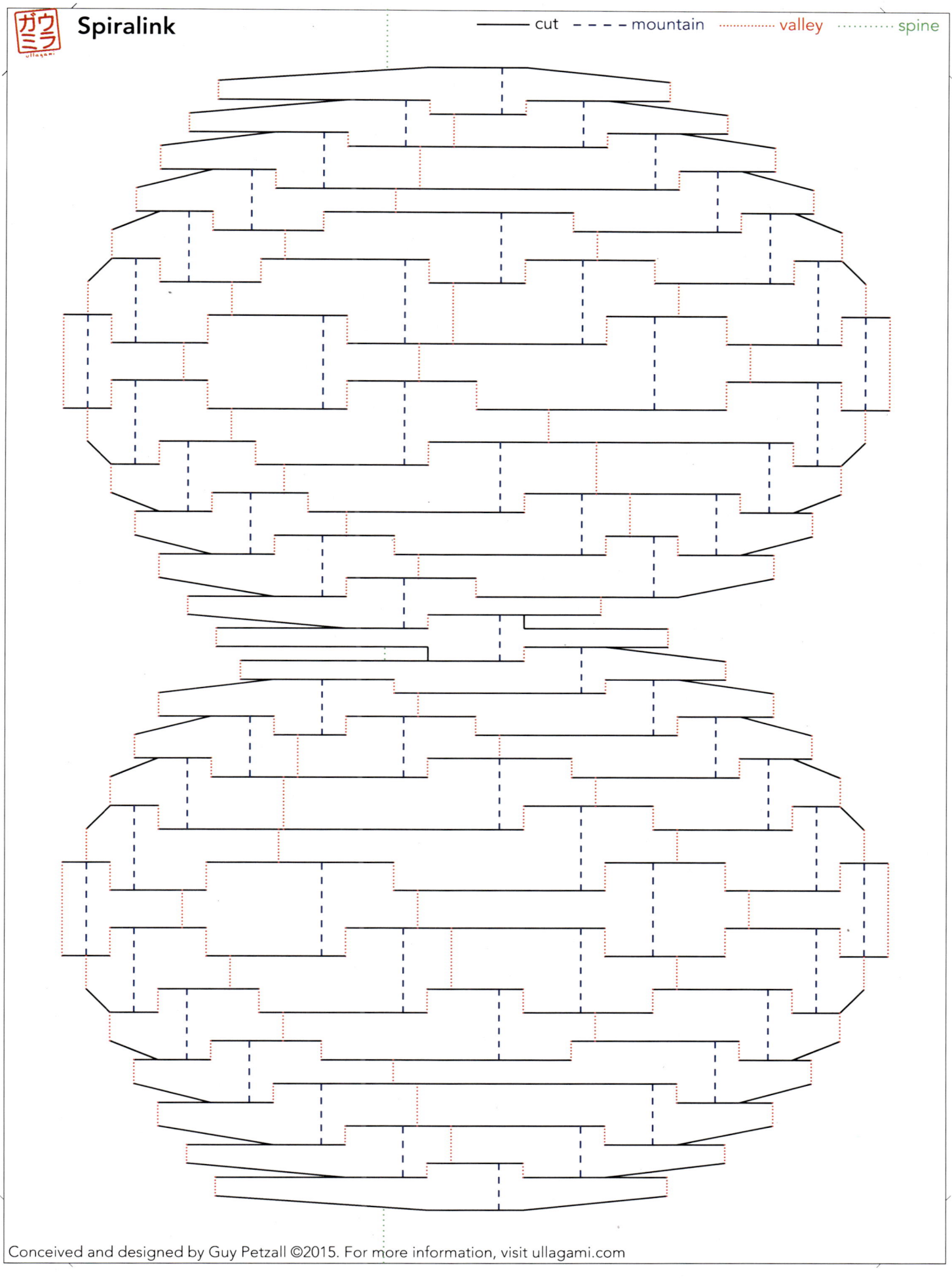

Big Spiralink

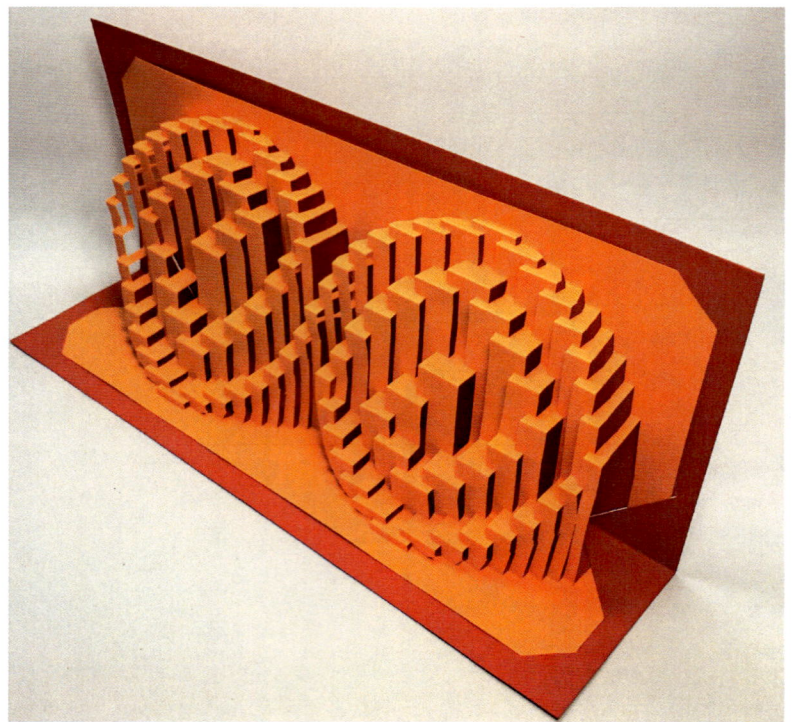

Go big or go home. Just like the spiralink, but in this case composed of 9x9 spirals, rather than 7x7.

This model is more challenging to construct. Many of the cuts and scores are only 2-3 mm wide, therefore some focused and deliberate presicion is required. The top- and bottom-most "single" blocks are the most difficult to fold; after that the rest collapses more easily.

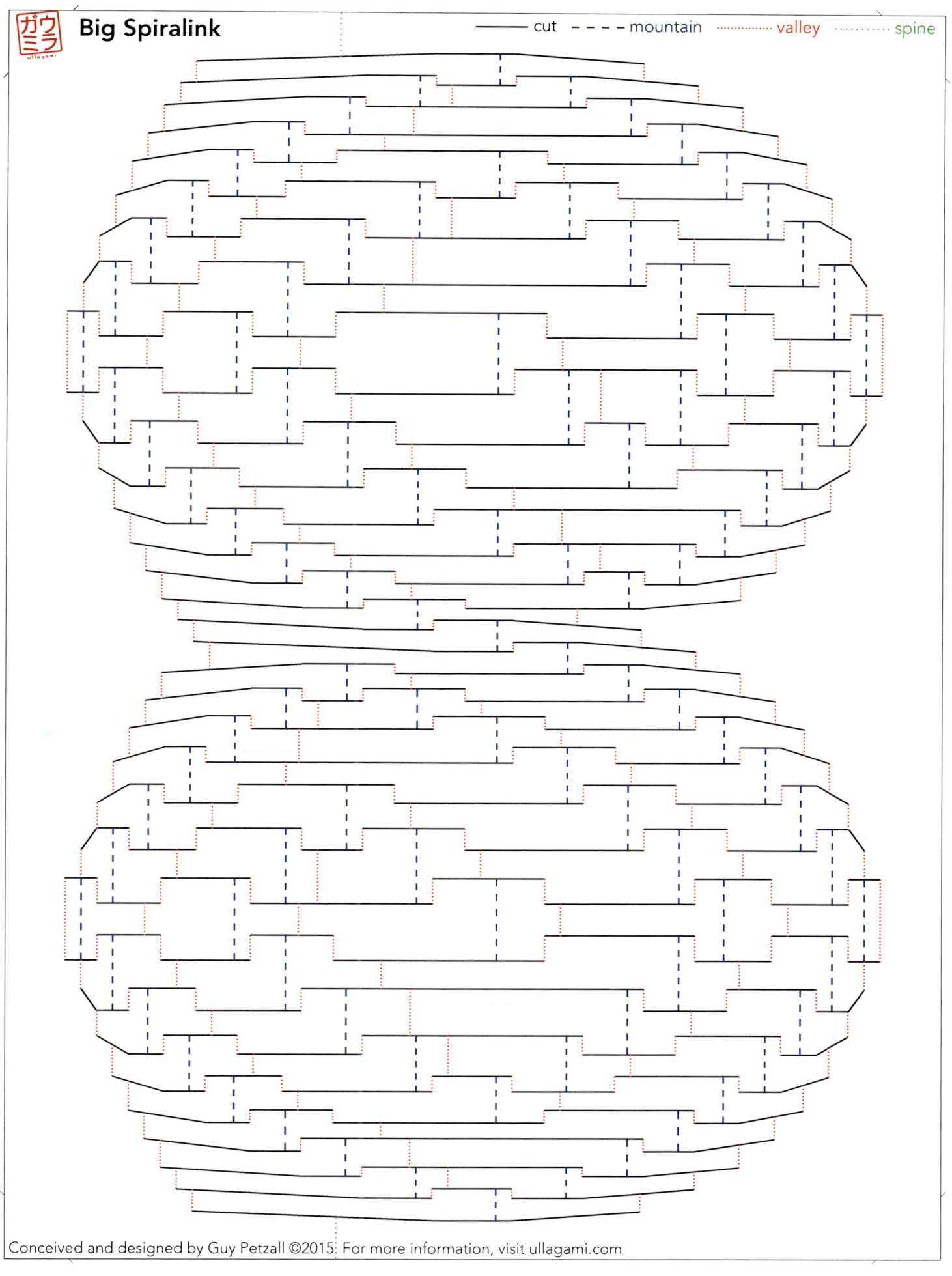

Eddies' Droop

Look familiar? This model is very similar to the Spiralink. The only difference is that, rather than having both spirals standing tall and shallow, here the second spiral reverses its slope, letting it droop down the page.

Then, to make it fit better on the sheet, the spine has been rotated 60°, adding to the peculiar symmetry of this design.

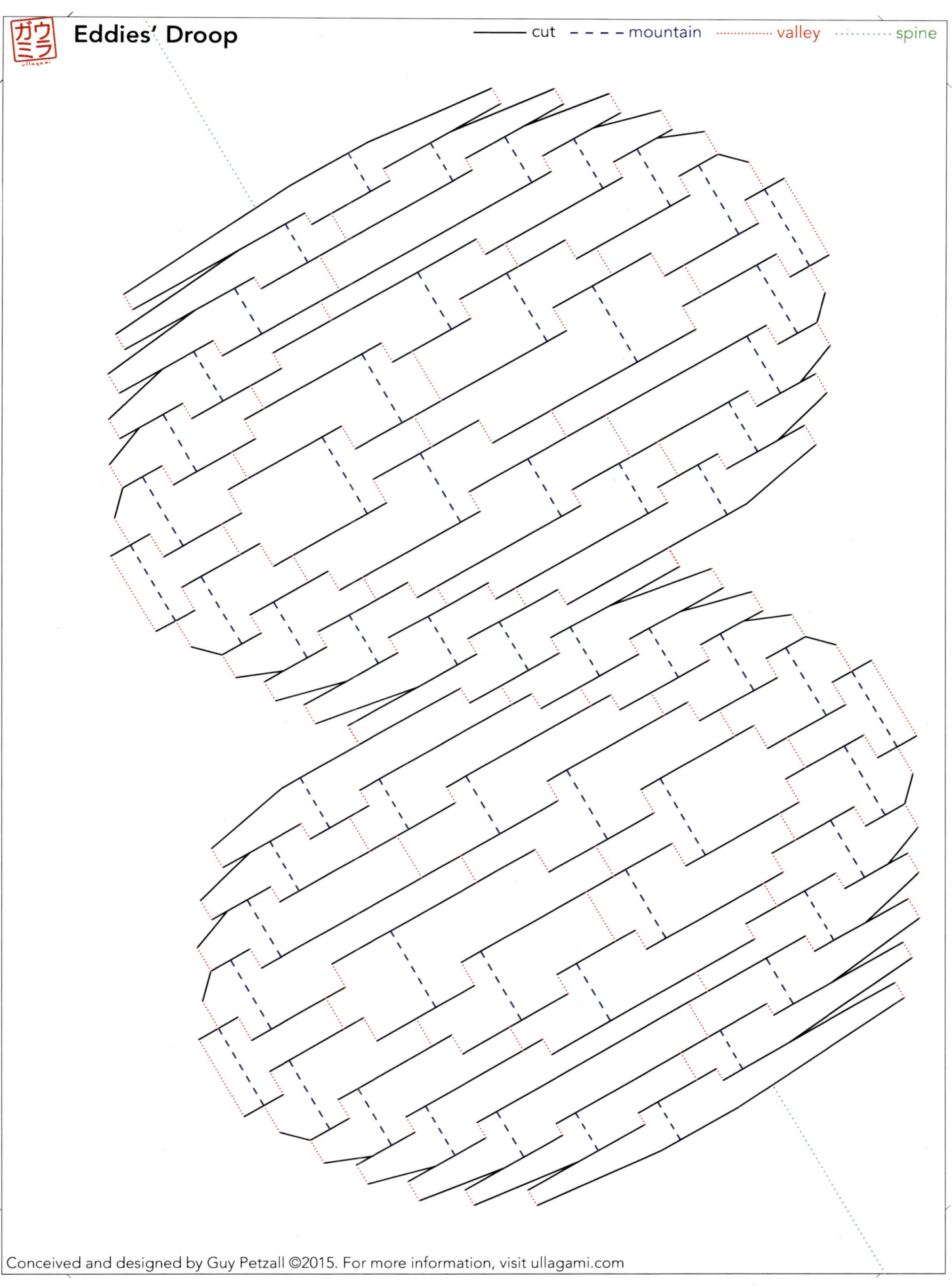

Made in United States
North Haven, CT
04 August 2022